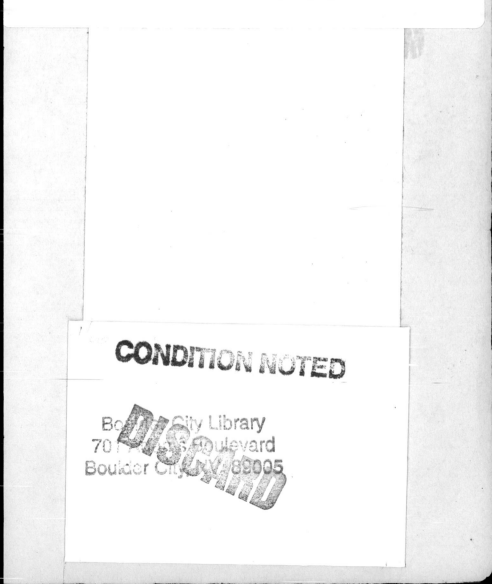

Amarillo Slim in a World Full of Fat People:
The Memoirs of the Greatest Gambler Who Ever Lived

AMARILLO SLIM'S

PLAY POKER

to

WIN

Million Dollar Strategies from the
Legendary World Series of Poker Winner

by AMARILLO SLIM PRESTON

◔ Collins

An Imprint of HarperCollinsPublishers

HarperCollins books may be purchased for educational, business, or
sales promotional use. For information please write: Special Markets
Department, HarperCollins Publishers, 10 East 53rd Street, New
York, NY 10022.

Originally published as *Play Poker to Win* in hardcover in 1973 by
Grosset & Dunlap.

First Collins edition published 2005

Designed by Emily Taff

Printed on acid-free paper

Library of Congress Cataloging-in-Publication Data

ISBN-10: 0-06-081755-0
ISBN-13: 978-0-06-081755-8

05 06 07 08 09 WBC/RRD 10 9 8 7 6 5 4 3 2 1

For Lorraine

"All you pay is the looking price. Lessons are extra."

—LANCEY HOWARD (Edward G. Robinson)
in the movie *The Cincinnati Kid*

CONTENTS

INTRODUCTION

Two thousand five hundred and seventy-six—that's how many people anted up $10,000 (or won their way in through a satellite) to play in the 2004 World Series of Poker. That's quite an increase from the eight players who competed in 1972 when I won the title. But don't misunderstand, partner, I'm not trying to say that my winning wasn't a big deal. Back then, the tournament itself wasn't much more than a publicity stunt, something my old pal Benny Binion created to put fannies in the seats—and, more important to him, to get people to gamble at his Horseshoe casino on Fremont Street in downtown Las Vegas. Back then we didn't need a tournament to tell us who the best player in the world was; we played all the time, and the best player was the one who won the most money, plain and simple.

That fellow with them funny sunglasses, Greg Raymer, who won in 2004, and that other cat named Moneymaker, who won in 2003, did an incredible thing by beating so many players. But even at age seventy-six, I'd lay a hundred to nothing that if I played either of them for a month straight, they'd end up scratching their broke ass. I've said over and over that poker is a game of skill in the long run with a lot of luck in the short run. Because a tournament takes place over a short period of time, luck plays a much greater factor.

Beginning in April 2003, the World Poker Tour launched its two-hour television show on the Travel Channel. My old buddy Lyle Berman is the brains behind that operation, which means it's no surprise to me that it's been a resounding success. It's currently the number-one-rated show on the network. And, of course, every year ESPN, the worldwide leader in sports, broadcasts the World Series of Poker from Binion's Horseshoe in Las Vegas. *Celebrity Poker Showdown* on Bravo managed to find a poker player taller than me to host the show (Phil Gordon), and people can't seem to get enough of it, either.

The producers of these shows figured out that if you want people to watch poker on television, they need to know what cards the players have. And that, my friends, might be the single biggest reason why poker has become so popular. When you watch football on TV, they don't show you the coaches' game plans or let you know what play the quarterback is about to call. But in poker, because you can see the hole cards, you can learn a lot about how a person plays—and the education is priceless.

And if you think televised poker is popular, turn on your computer and see what's happening online. I once owned a computer and nearly threw it clear through the window. I'm a people person, so it's not for me, but I'm told that PokerStars.com has 1.3 million registered users and they're not even number one in the market. That honor belongs to PartyPoker.com, which I'm told made somewhere in the neighborhood of $300 million last year.

I guess what I'm trying to tell you, neighbor, is that poker has come of age, and there has never been a better time for you to get fat in the hip. There are games all over the world and no shortage of bad players. That's why I figured it was time for me to update this book.

———

I play poker to win.

I've been doing that in places all over the world for years. It's the way I make my living—I'm a professional gambler—and I've won and lost millions of dollars at the poker table; but at seventy-six, I'm still playing, so I must have won more than I lost.

I won the World Series of Poker in Las Vegas, Nevada, in May 1972, and, neighbor, at one point I had a better chance of getting a French date with the Statue of Liberty than I did of winning that tournament. In fact, with $80,000 on the table divided between the remaining players in that elimination game, I was down at one time to $1,700, while a spectator behind the rail was betting 25 to 1 that I wouldn't win. Of course, I took that bet. It gave me incentive, but I really didn't need any more with all of those black $100 *chips* already on the table. A little later, I graduated to being an 8 to 5 underdog, and I took some of that, too.

I've played poker in every sizable city in the United States, and in just about every casino and elite private club in Europe, Asia, and South America. I go anywhere for a big game because I thrive on action. Don't get me wrong—I like the money, too—but it's the challenge and thrill of matching wits with and beating the best poker players in the world that turns me on.

A wire-service reporter once described me as a "walking encyclopedia of what's going on in gaming circles." I guess that's true, but another newspaperman caught my exact feelings when he wrote in a story about me: "He plays constantly, devotedly, joyously, wholeheartedly, and with passion—as certain consecrated artists practice their art." He might have added that poker is my nourishment: My six-foot-four, 171-pound frame, which long ago earned me the nickname of "Slim," doesn't require much actual grub to keep it going.

I make no bones about being a pro, and the men I gamble with are pros: the cream-of-the-crop blue-ribbon players—tops in their fields whether it's Omaha, stud, or Hold'em. Nowadays, of course, it seems like all everyone wants to play is No Limit Hold'em. It's no surprise because it's always been the favored game in Texas, and my buddy Doyle Brunson calls No Limit Hold'em the "Cadillac" of poker games.

The same principles of play followed by the pros who you see on television also apply if you're playing in the average American weekend poker session, in the home, online, at the Indian reservation, at the local Elks Club, or at the country club.

Sure, the power of the *cold bluff* is restricted in a game with a limit. But things such as psychology, *position*, basic probability, spotting a *"tell,"* and *trapping* (and all trappers don't wear fur caps) are just as important for the players in a home game as for the pros at the World Series in Las Vegas. I don't mention hunches because I don't believe in them; hunches are for dogs making love.

I was a pool hustler before I was a poker player. It was a hell of a good education for what was yet to come, not to mention that it made me some money. I became the champion snooker player in my hometown, and later I traveled around the globe, beating some of the best in the business, including a man named Rudolph Walderone, who we used to call New York Fats and later became better known as Minnesota Fats. But since pool wasn't lucrative for very long after World War II, I changed my focus to poker.

Poker was an offshoot of my pool-shooting days. Not all gamblers who hang around pool halls bet on the pool games, you know. That's how I started playing cards in my late teens, because

I'm a dude who likes to bet on anything competitive. In fact, if there's anything I'll argue about, I'll either bet on it or shut up. And since it's not very becoming for a cowboy to be arguing, I've made a few wagers in my day.

In my memoir, which I titled *Amarillo Slim in a World Full of Fat People*—and by fat I mean fat in the hip—I wrote about all of my proposition bets over the years. I've bet big money that I could broad jump farther than anybody on a golf course, that I could pick any thirty people at random and two of them would have the same birthday, and that a stray cat that wandered into a swank club was so smart he could carry an empty Coke bottle across the room and set it on the cash register. I beat Willie Nelson for $300,000 playing dominoes right on Fremont Street in downtown Las Vegas. I took Minnesota Fats for big money playing pool—with a broom. And I won too many wagers from Evel Knievel to remember, but the one everyone likes to talk about is the time I beat that old daredevil in golf when I played with a carpenter's hammer.

The truth is that I had to rely on these proposition bets because all of the town's poker studs regularly beat the hell out of me during the early days. Those guys would break me every week, but I was learning, neighbor. And practical experience is the best experience. Back then, I'd lose my ass pushing A-K when I didn't even flop a pair, but I learned to adjust to my mistakes.

There have been some good books written on poker, but most of them have been by college professors, or by people who have run something through computers. The advice that I have to offer on how to play smart, winning poker comes from thousands of hours spent at the poker tables, with big, big money at stake.

I had to learn to use my eyes and my ears, and, neighbor, I can see a gnat's keister at a hundred yards and hear a mouse piss on cotton. I'm also pretty good with head arithmetic, which some people call percentages and odds. But most important of all, I have learned to like and to know people. I can go back anywhere I've ever played.

Today, there are more card players in America than there are golfers, bowlers, and tennis players combined. In fact, the *New York Times* recently estimated that 70 million Americans play poker, and it doesn't require that much sense for you to be better than 99 percent of them. My old friend Eric Drache used to joke that he was the seventh-best player in the world, and let me tell you that boy could play. His problem, as he described while he was scratching his broke ass, was that he only played against the top six. And partner, there's a lesson in that for you.

If you go to Vegas looking to match wits against the world's best, like Doyle, Chip Reese, and Johnny Chan, they'll eat you up like ginger cake. Sure, to be a *world-class player*, you're going to need to take your licks against the best players in the world at some point, but if you want to be a winning player, all you need is to be world class, *relative* to your opponents. That's another way of saying that you can't let ego get in the way. If you want to make money playing poker, selecting the right game is the most important factor. As Warren Buffett and a million other fellows have said, "If you can't find the sucker at the table, you're it."

The following pages contain the lessons I've learned in some of the world's biggest poker games. It's information you can put to use next Saturday night and come out a winner. In the frontier days, a man's word was good enough for deals involving thousands of dollars, and it's still that way in our circle. That's why I think one of the biggest reasons for my later success in poker was that I learned to like and to know people. I can go back anywhere I've ever played, because I've always kept my promises. A gambler's word is his bond. If one of them boys tells you a goose'll pull a plow a hundred yards, then hook him up, neighbor, 'cause he'll damn sure move it out.

DESCRIPTION *of* GAMES *and* GENERAL STRATEGY

Just as pool has eight ball, nine ball, straight pool, and one-pocket, poker has draw, stud, lowball, Texas Hold'em, Omaha, and a million varieties in between—not to mention online poker and tournaments. In the pages that follow, I'll be giving you advice on all those games, and for you folks who like to play at home, I've even included a chapter on poker games with wild cards and all those other crazy games that your Aunt Mary likes to play around the kitchen table.

If you're completely new to the game, I've included a list of hand rankings in the appendix on page 179.

Five-card draw is the game that most poker players—at least those born before 1980—learn first. You get five cards, bet, and then get to draw cards followed by another betting round. A variety of five-card draw is called deuce-to-seven lowball, or "Kansas City" lowball. It works the same as regular draw except the best possible hand is the worst in regular poker: 2-3-4-5-7 of different suits. Ace is high, and straights and flushes count against you.

Five-card stud was a popular game up until about 1960, but the only game you'll find now is between Lancey Howard (Edward G. Robinson) and Eric Stoner (Steve McQueen) if you rent a video of *The Cincinnati Kid*. In five-card stud, each player gets one card dealt facedown and one card dealt faceup after the ante. There's a round of betting before the next three cards are dealt faceup, one at a time, with a betting round after each.

Seven-card stud is similar except each player starts with two cards down and one up, and after three cards are dealt faceup with a round of betting after each, the seventh and final card is dealt facedown. Up until the World Poker Tour was televised in 2003, stud was the most popular game on the East Coast at places like Foxwoods in Connecticut or the Taj Mahal in Atlantic City. Seven-card stud can also be played for the best low hand, and that game is called razz. You'll also see it played quite a bit as hi-lo split.

While all these other poker games are okay and all, as far as I'm concerned, there's just one real form of poker: Texas Hold'em. And as the expression goes, I could teach you to play in a day, but it would take you a lifetime to learn. The game can be played with as many as twenty-three players, but most games are usually played with between seven and ten players. For me, the fewer the better, and I like nothing better than playing one-person "heads-up."

Here's how the game works: Each player is dealt two cards followed by a round of betting. If you're dealt two aces, you've got the boss hand—for the time being anyway. The dealer then *flops* three *community cards* in the middle that everyone can use to make their hand, followed by a round of betting. Then comes the fourth card, called the *turn* or *fourth street*, followed by a round of betting. Then—and this is where many a man has been drowned—comes the fifth community card, which is called the *river* or *fifth street*, which is followed by the fourth and last round of betting.

Omaha is a variety of Hold'em, with the only difference being that you get dealt four cards, and instead of using five of the best seven cards to make your hand, you use five of the best nine to make your hand (and you must use two from your hand and three from the board). You rarely see Hold'em played hi-lo, but it's pretty common to play Omaha that way. Whoever makes the high hand gets half the pot and whoever makes the low gets the other half. The place where you really make your money is when you make both and "scoop" or "hog" the pot, which can happen when you have four cards in your hand.

♠ BETTING LIMITS

Aside from all the varieties of games, what really matters more than anything are the rules of betting. Most friendly games across America and most games in casinos are fixed limit—nickel-dime, $1–$2, or $10–$20—where you must bet and raise a set amount on each round of betting. The power of a pure bluff is restricted in a game with a limit.

Here in Texas, and for all the major tournaments, the betting is no limit, meaning you can bet anything that's in front of you at any time, or pot limit, meaning you can bet the amount in the pot at any time. Don't get me wrong, limit poker can be a lot of fun—if you haven't got the guts of an earthworm or if you don't make your living as an accountant. As far as I'm concerned, if you can't *"move in"* on someone—meaning bet everything you've got in front of you—then it's not real poker. So, naturally, No Limit

Texas Hold'em is my game of choice, and it's what is played to determine the winner of the World Series of Poker.

♥ BASIC STRATEGY

If you could choose only two words to describe the poker greats, they would have to be *tight* and *aggressive*. They are "tight" in that they don't play many hands and play only when they have an edge. They are "aggressive" in that when they do have the edge, they will bet heavily. Now, if you watch players like Gus Hansen and Phil Ivey on TV, you're probably saying that there's nothing tight about their play. It almost seems as if they're playing *every* hand, which isn't so far from the truth. The reason they can play a lot of hands is that they are so good at reading other players that they can outplay them after the flop.

Keep in mind that the poker you see on TV is no limit and those are two of the best players in the world. It's basic common sense that in the long run whoever *starts* with the best hand is going to *finish* with the best hand. As a beginner, your advantage over other novices is being selective—you won't put money in the pot unless you have something, while they'll chase with anything just to be involved. So you want to be very tight at first. Poker is about maximizing your wins and minimizing your losses, and playing good cards allows you to do both.

As you get better and become more confident in reading your opponents, you'll be able to loosen up a bit and play more hands because you'll know how to get away from them when you're beat and how to milk your opponent like a Rocky Mountain goat when you've got the best of it.

So while it's debatable how tight you should play, it's not even a question if you should be aggressive. All the winning players are aggressive. This is going to sound so simple, but write it down and take a picture of it if you have to:

If you bet (or raise), you have two ways to win—everyone folds or you have the best hand. If you call, the only way you can win is if you have the best hand.

Players who call are just hoping to win. When a player bets in front of you, as far as I'm concerned, your two choices are to pump it or dump it. Pump it—meaning raise—if you think you've got the best of it, or dump it—meaning fold—if you don't. Sure, every now and then calling is the appropriate play, but it happens a lot less than you think.

If you're going to be a winning player, you need to be aggressive. It's as simple as that.

♣ GAME SELECTION

Before I would drive to a game in Texas, the first thing I would do was call the boss running the game and find out who was playing. If there were more people in the game who were there *to gamble*, and not *to win*, it was time to play. If the game was full of a bunch of other professionals, I'd be content to stay home. Don't be one of those fools who needs to get his fix and will play in any game. Save your energy for those times when you're a *favorite* to win.

In a casino, I'll go from table to table and study the action. The first thing I'm looking for is *un*familiar faces. Chances are that if I don't know a person, he isn't that good. The people I do recognize like Doyle Brunson are not people I want to play with. Not to say that I couldn't put a licking on my old buddy, but why would I when there are so many easier marks?

I take game selection very seriously. If I spot a buddy at a table, I'll pull him aside and ask him how the game's going and try to get a report on unknown players. If my buddy says, "Seat seven is tighter than a nun's gadget," I know that I can bluff him out of the pot all day long.

The floorperson is another great resource, because he or she knows the players better than anyone. Since most poker players don't bother to tip this person, throw him a couple of chips and he's liable to tell you which game to play in.

Poker is a treacherous game. That's why if I can't find the sucker at the table—or even better, three or four suckers—I will switch tables or go home. Poker is such a complex game that you'll need to play thousands of hours before you become an expert, and you still may never become one. But what you can do to become a *winning* player almost immediately is to find players who play worse than you and wait for them to make mistakes. Becoming a *world-class player* is tough, but if you want to be a *winning* player, all you need to do is sit at a table with players who don't play as well as you.

If you're going out of your way to find the tough players to test yourself, you'll quickly be finding your way to the broke house.

I can't say this enough times:

The biggest factor in your success is game selection. The biggest factor in your demise will be your ego.

Along the lines of game selection is seat selection. I also make it a practice to move seats whenever I can. I want aggressive players on my right so I can either get out of their way or reraise when they make a play for the pot. Just as important, I want tight players on my left. If I can find two passive players seated next to each other, I will move to their immediate left so I can steal their *blinds*.

♦ QUITTING WINNERS

I know a guy named Hammer who is known for being a "hit-and-run" artist; the minute he wins a little money he hits the door. I hear him say all the time that you can't argue with a win. When he's losing, I'll hear him vow to quit as soon as he gets *even*. And those are the times that he ends up playing marathon sessions and blowing his entire bankroll.

How many times have you sold a stock that has appreciated and said to yourself, "You can't go broke taking a gain," only to see that stock skyrocket just after you've sold it? Even worse, how many times have you held a stock that's gone down, waiting to "get even" before you sold it, and then turn around and watch that stock go down to almost nothing? If you're human, this probably happens to you a lot.

Common sense dictates that when things are going well, you should keep playing and take advantage of your momentum. It would also seem to make sense that when you are struggling, you should take a small loss and come back another day. But in poker, it goes beyond common sense. When you're winning, you have a psychological edge on your opponents, and when you're losing, they have one on you.

I believe that with very few exceptions, every poker player in the world is a worse player after he has lost his first buy-in. In no limit, I think this rule applies fiftyfold for the simple reason that you cannot win while being passive.

If you want to be a winner in poker, you have to be able to quit a loser. That's worth repeating: *If you want to be a winner in poker, you have to be able to quit a loser.* And damn it, I know that walking away from the poker table with a loss is one of the hardest things in the world to do. It's also the most important thing you can do if you want to hang on to your bankroll. And for goodness sake, when you get ahead, that's the time to keep playing!

♠ WALK IN YOUR OPPONENTS' SHOES

Here's a quick quiz.

You are playing seven-card stud, and all the cards have been dealt to all the players. Each player has three hidden cards and four cards showing. You are *showing* four aces. What you have in the hole doesn't matter, since the only hand that can beat you is a straight flush.

Everyone has folded except for one opponent who is showing 5-6-7-8—all hearts. Since you are showing the highest hand with four aces, you have to act first, and you have two choices. You can bet or check (pass). If you're an amateur, your first reaction is to think, "Holy cow, four aces is a great hand, so I'm going to bet." But then you look over at your opponent's hand and stop to think. If your opponent has the four or nine of hearts in the hole, he has a straight flush, which beats your four aces. If he has a nine of a different suit, he has a straight, which doesn't beat four aces. If he has a different heart, he has a flush, which doesn't beat you, either.

So even if he has a straight or a flush, it makes sense to bet, right? Before you automatically say yes, think about it for a second, partner. Your opponent is looking at your hand and *sees* four aces. If you bet and your opponent does in fact have a straight flush, he is going to raise you. And even if he only has a straight or a flush (or nothing), it doesn't beat the four aces he's looking at, so he is going to fold.

So here you are sitting with four aces and there isn't any way in the world you can make any money on this betting round. Unless of course, you have some sense.

You see, if you check, your opponent might try to bluff. If you bet, he might raise you even if he doesn't have you beat—hoping to make you think that he has a straight flush so you'll fold. Knowing which to do depends on how you read your opponent, and there isn't an easy answer.

Abraham Lincoln said, "When I am getting ready to reason with a man, I spend one-third of my time thinking about myself and what I am going to say, and two-thirds thinking about him and what he is going to say."

If Old Abe were teaching you poker, he'd be telling you, neighbor, that *your ability to make money in poker has very little to do with your own cards.* It's strictly a function of knowing your opponent. You must see the hand from his perspective in order to win money from him. Bad players play their own hand. Good ones play their opponents' hand first, then worry about their own cards.

Your hand in poker is only good *relative* to the hand of your opponents. Four aces isn't worth nine settings of eggs if your opponent has a straight flush. On the other hand, a pair of deuces is like the world's fair if you know your opponent doesn't have anything. It almost seems too obvious to say, but if you're going to be a great poker player, you need to walk in the shoes of your opponents. You need to think about what they're holding, what they're thinking, and what they think you're thinking!

♥ AMARILLO SLIM'S
TOP-TEN KEYS TO POKER SUCCESS

I'm not the type of fellow who is going to piss on your leg and tell you it's raining. Poker isn't a simple game, and if you want to become an expert, you'll need to play tens of thousands of hours, study every book and software program you can get your hands on, and find good mentors who can talk you through hands. I know all you owls out there think that you're a natural, but if you're naive enough to believe that you don't need to work at getting better, then I reckon you're familiar with the ridiculous vig that the loan sharks are charging these days.

When I was writing my memoir, I took a break to watch that old hoot David Letterman and came up with a top-ten list of my own on the secrets to poker. So while I'm going to get into some advanced concepts later, I want to start out by giving you a quick list with some of the simplest and most important advice on poker.

1. Play the players more than you play the cards.
2. Choose the right opponents. If you don't see a sucker at the table, you're it.
3. Never play with money you can't afford to lose.
4. Be tight and aggressive; don't play many hands, but when you do, be prepared to move in.
5. Always be observing at a poker game. The minute you're there, you're working.
6. Watch the other players for "tells" before you look at your own cards.
7. Diversify your play so other players can't pick up tells on you.

⑧ Choose your speed based on the direction of the game. Play slow in a *fast game* and fast in a slow game.

⑨ Be able to quit a loser, and for goodness sake, keep playing when you're winning.

⑩ Conduct yourself honorably so you're always invited back.

That's a nice list and all, but if you could master the first item on that list, it's the only thing you'll ever need: Play the *players* more than you play the *cards*. What they say is true: A man's eyes mirror his soul. Why do you think I always wear a big-old brimmed Stetson when I play? A man's eyes show 90 percent of what he's thinking. When I'm wearing my hat, you can only see my eyes when I want you to. Besides what you can see from a person's eyes, you also can pick up something about his hand from other physical giveaways, known among poker players as tells.

TELLS

$\mathcal{M}$ ike Caro has made quite a name for himself as the "Mad Genius of Poker," but back when we used to treat him like a stepchild, everyone I knew called him Crazy Mike. And boy, let me tell you, I don't think his elevator has ever gone all the way to the top. But just because he's crazy, it doesn't mean he isn't smart. In fact, he wrote an exceptional book on reading people at the poker table called *Caro's Book of Tells*. He also was a contributor to Doyle Brunson's book *Doyle Brunson's Super System: A Course in Power Poker*, in which he wrote:

> These people—the majority of folks you meet every day—are actors. They present themselves to you as people different than they really are.
>
> Deep within themselves they know they are not the same people they pretend to be. On an unconscious level, they think, "Hey, I'm so phony that if I don't act to disguise my poker hand, everyone will see right through me!"

And that's why the majority of these pitiful people are going to give you their money by always acting weak when they're strong and strong when they're weak.

The word "tell" comes from the word "telegraph"—meaning to give away or make obvious. In poker, a tell gives away information about a player's hand. In the movie *Rounders*, Mike (Matt Damon) detects a tell from Teddy KGB (John Malkovich) based on the way he eats his Oreo cookies. Something as subtle as the way a player sits in his chair or throws his chips in the pot may give you an indication of the player's hand.

In his book, Caro did a great job of explaining that typically in poker, weak is strong and strong is weak. When your opponent is looking away from you, trying not to be noticed, he probably has a great hand and is trying to appear weak, so you will call (see the bet) and add to his pot. The opponent who is staring you down, trying to intimidate you by appearing strong, is usually bluffing and is trying to get you to fold. Even simpler, a player who is talking is usually bluffing, and one who is silent typically isn't.

You see this premise played out all the time in everyday life. Take the guy who is quick to tell you how he is making money "hand over fist"—it's a good bet that he's been trying to borrow from everyone in the room. It's simple human nature that we overcompensate for our weaknesses by displaying strength.

At the highest levels of poker, in which all the players know the basic premise that weak is strong and strong is weak, it can also be used as a reverse tactic. A player will sometimes try to intimidate an opponent by acting strong so that the other player will think, "Strong must be weak," but all along, the player was just setting his opponent up and really was holding a strong hand. But in the lower-stakes games, weak usually is strong and strong usually is weak.

Mike Caro's Great Law of Tells states: "Players are either acting or they aren't. If they are acting, then decide what they want you to do and disappoint them."

♣ SPOTTING TELLS

Go to any cardroom and watch a high-stakes poker game. Study a professional player and you'll notice that when the cards are dealt, he watches his opponents to see their immediate reaction before he bothers to look at his own cards. If an opponent winces in disgust when he looks at his cards, the pro has picked up a valuable tell and knows that he can bet and win the pot—whether he has a good hand or not.

What that means is you shouldn't be the sucker who stares at the flop. Let me let you in on a little secret, neighbor: The flop isn't going to change if you wait a few seconds to look at it! When the flop comes, you can either look at your opponents to get a read on their reaction, or stare at the flop and let them get a read on you.

One player may talk a lot if he's got a hand, giving signs of being anxious to raise; while another player may become very quiet if he's holding something. I can say this now because he's no longer alive, but Jack "Treetop" Strauss, a world-class player who won the World Series in 1982, whistled ever so quietly when he was bluffing. Shoot, neighbor, if you can pick up a tell like that on somebody, he might as well be playing with his hand faceup.

Tony Holden, that author who called me the Imelda Marcos of poker, described in his book *Big Deal* how I use words to pick up tells from my opponents.

Amarillo Slim is one of poker's great talkers. This is not just his natural joie de vivre. Table talk, to Slim, is a wily tactic, designed to throw his opponents off their game. Variations on such themes as "Hey, neighbor, you better not call that big bet o' mine, ah got six little titties (three queens) down here," or "This man's slower than a mule with three broken legs," or (if there are no ladies present) "This sucker's tighter than a nun's doodah," have won Slim a handsome fortune for years, and helped him become the most celebrated poker player of his time.

♦ THE TELL IS IN THE TEA

While he was in Vegas, drug lord Jimmy Chagra would play golf for half a million dollars a round and once tipped a cocktail waitress $10,000 for bringing him a bottle of water. Treetop said about Chagra's time in Las Vegas: "It was like having that TV program *Fantasy Island*. I kept waiting for Tattoo to come on and say it was all a dream: 'Look, boss! The plane! The plane!' " Chagra always wanted to beat me at something, so after I had fleeced him on the golf course and at the poker table enough times, he got a hold of Betty Carey to play me in a head-up poker game at the Las Vegas Hilton. Betty, an attractive woman from Cody, Wyoming, was the most aggressive player I've ever played against. She was also regarded as the best woman player in the world, and there ain't no question she was. Jimmy staked her $100,000 to play me head-up in a No Limit Texas Hold'em *freeze-out*, which is our word for winner takes all.

We sat down to play and gave our money to the *floorman*, who went to get our chips. Betty and I are were just sitting at the table with the dealer and the hangers-on, who were sucking around the *rail* and all, waiting for old Slim to get shown up by a nice little lady.

I was drinking coffee, which I usually did when I played, and I said, "Betty, I'm gonna have some more coffee. Would you like some?"

"No, thank you, Slim," she said, "but I will have some hot tea."

I wasn't thinking anything of it at the time, about how she said it, but as a poker player, you're *always* working, trying to learn just the smallest thing about an opponent that might make the difference in a big pot. Well, it took a while to get the cards and count out $200,000 worth of chips, and I finished my coffee and, just real casual, asked, "Betty, how is your tea?"

"Oh, wonderful," she said, "this is real good tea."

And I knew she liked it. She had no reason to lie; it wasn't like she needed to convince me that the tea at the Las Vegas Hilton was just as good as the Queen Mother's. She could have been drinking rat piss as far as I was concerned, but the way she said she liked that tea, that got me to thinking. So I thought, "Well, after a while I'll ask her something else and see how she answers."

About an hour later, a big pot came up—one that was so big a show dog couldn't jump over it—and she moved in on me. Here she was risking all her chips, and I smelled a bluff. I just didn't think she had anything, so just like we were having a normal conversation, I said to her, "Betty, how do you like your hand?"

"Real good hand, Slim," she said, but the tone of her voice was just a little bit different than when I had asked her about the tea. It lacked the same sincerity. Now I knew she was a lying ass! I knew that her answer about the tea was sincere, and this one wasn't. So I called her with a lousy pair of fives—and I won the pot. She didn't disappoint me one bit: she had nothing and had been making a stone-cold bluff.

After I won, I bragged to everyone there that a woman would have a better chance of putting a wildcat in a tobacco sack than she would of beating me at poker.

Of course, that only made Betty want to beat me more, and the next time I played her, again it was a $100,000 freeze-out, Jimmy staked her on the condition that she wore earplugs. Boy, that was hard—talking to my opponents is my secret weapon, and I couldn't get much of a read on her or pick up any tells from her voice. Sure enough, she busted my skinny ass and made me eat my words. See what I mean about playing the *players* more than you play the *cards*?

What sets the experts in poker apart from their competition is their ability to read people and understand the tells of their opponents. Without this skill, a good player will remain merely good. With this skill, a good player becomes a legend.

PSYCHOLOGY of SMART POKER

$\mathcal{P}$sychology is a fancy word, but you don't
have to be a licensed psychologist to practice it in poker.

I'll give you an example of applied psychology. Ironically, it
happened when I wasn't playing poker. As I've said before, I've
been known to speculate on anything that's competitive.

One day, I was playing golf with some gambling buddies in Amarillo, Texas, where I grew up and still live today. Among the golfers
was Big Jim, who always was thinking up something different to bet
on, especially with me. Big Jim turns to me and, taking the tooth-
pick he is chewing out of his mouth, says, "Slim, you think you can
outrun anybody that's here on the golf course right now?"

"You're goddamn right I think I can, buddy." You can see I
have never been shy, and I did have a reputation for being a fairly
fleet-of-foot cat. In fact, I had outrun some good athletes on past
occasions when money was riding on the outcome. I once even

ran a footrace with a quarter horse, which is about equal to racing the wind; and I won it, too.

Although we continue to play golf for a while longer, I can hear the wheels turning in Big Jim's head. I also notice that Big Jim's caddy is a long-legged, loose-jointed kid who floats on his feet and impresses me as being able to outrun a gazelle.

I begin to limp a little. "Damn it, Jim," I say. "I hurt my heel somehow on that last hole. I don't think I can run a race. But I tell you what: I'll bet you that I can broad jump farther than anyone on the links right now—you name him!"

"You really think so, huh?" Big Jim hitches up his pants and gets kind of a dirty, cat-that-ate-the-canary grin on his face. He glances at his stilt-legged-kid caddy, and adds, "Okay, you're on." Then he steps away a few feet and draws a line on the grass. "This will be the jumping line," he says.

"Hold on a minute, partner," I interrupt. "Since this is a golf course, let's jump from behind a golf club." As I say this, I lay down an iron.

"Why the hell you want to use a golf club?" Big Jim asks. He's trying to figure if I've got a gimmick, and if I do, what kind.

"I just think it's more in keeping with the surroundings. What's it they say—when in Rome, do as the Romans. I've also got a stipulation that's got to be made before this is a bet: If either jumper even *touches* this golf club, he's disqualified and loses the money. All right?"

Big Jim doesn't see anything wrong with that, so he nods in agreement. Now, it doesn't take a Nobel Prize–winning scientist to figure out that Big Jim's entry will be this caddy of his. While I limber up a little, getting ready for the big jump, Big Jim and his buddies are huddling close by, pooling their money to make additional wagers. I sidle up to this caddy, who looks to me as though he could jump farther than a goosed frog. I bend over to tighten my shoelaces, saying to him in a low voice:

"Let me give you some friendly advice, kid. Big Jim and those friends of his are tough babies, and if you accidentally lose them a bundle of money, why, my god, they're just as liable to kick your ass all the way down to the creek and back. Of course, if you lose because I outjump you, that's a horse of a different color—but just don't accidentally touch that golf club!"

I move off without waiting for him to say anything as Big Jim comes up to talk to the kid. The kid's eyes are getting as big as basketballs. A few of Big Jim's words waft over on the breeze: ". . . and if you do, you little bastard, I'll stomp the hell out of you!"

We flip a coin to see who jumps first, and I'm the one.

I get a good start and give it all I got when I spring, making pretty good distance, which is then marked.

Now I watch the kid. It looks as if he's dropped back a whole city block. Then he's running like hell—he's just a blur, and I'm very glad I'm not racing him. Suddenly he leaves the ground, a good two yards behind that golf club! Even then it looks to me like he's going into orbit. When he comes down, even after that two-yard safety margin he took, he's barely a few inches behind my jump. I collect the money, but, neighbor, I'd never have won it without a little applied psychology.

I learned how to use psychology in poker. Using it, you have an edge that can make the difference between winning and losing. In fact, as I'll continue to tell you, I play the *players* more than I play the *cards*.

If you're going to win the money, psychology is as important as position at the table, the odds and percentages involved in making a hand, knowing how to *figure the price of the pot*, or running a trap.

Good poker psychology is based on two things: intelligent observation and common sense. Psychology also calls for old-fashioned ham-acting and high-pressure salesmanship. If you put it all together right, you'll win at poker, whether it is the weekend family game or a high-stakes game at Bellagio.

However, it goes almost without saying that you *must* know the people you are playing poker with; if you don't know them, you'd better start studying them, because if you really know and understand your fellow card players, you can decide how to play your hand even before the turn of the cards. Knowing how the other players play is a fundamentally sharp poker strategy.

Appearances count for everything, neighbor. I clown when I'm playing (except in Merry Old England, where they have rules against it). Because of the tells that most amateurs or part-time poker players have, I wouldn't give you a plugged nickel to stand behind these players and call out their hands. They are already telling me through their actions what they're holding.

Avoid being stereotyped yourself. Don't be a "nine-to-five" type of player; instead, vary your style, mix up your play. If you play the same way all the time, then your tells become obvious to sharp players.

For example, if I'm playing stud with a man who's been waiting to catch an ace, a king, a queen, or a jack in the hole, I'll beat that cat. You don't have to play with someone like that very long before you see the kind of hand he's *showing down* and the kind of cards that he is playing back at you with. I am more prone to catch a six in the hole and try to make a couple of sixes. With good players around the table, you're liable to sell them those two sixes for a lot. And the idea is to sell your hand real high if you make it; you've had to pay something to make it, so sell it as high as you can, because the next one you draw, you are liable to miss.

If you're a tight player, you will tell me that by your bets and your way of playing what you're holding. So the next time you are playing stud and get an ace in the hole and another ace hits you, play it easy. Stall a little before you call a bet: Act like you're wondering if you can win it with an ace high; if you've been playing tight for some time, this can work to your advantage by setting up a trap. The reason is that I will know you as a tight player, and you come in and make a pair of sixes. When a six hits, I don't pay any attention; based on your past method of playing, I don't think the six will help you any. Therefore, you can trap me; you may bust me with that hand. I'm liable to call you with my ace high because I'll put you down as having a king, a queen, or a jack in the hole; I won't be looking for those two sixes that beat me. Your trap has snapped closed. So beware of falling into a play pattern.

The psychology of a loser is a funny thing, and the majority of these gamblers are losers. I believe that losing is for the tourists and the suckers. But it seems that most folks would *rather* lose than win; it is as though they are trying to make some kind of sacrifice, to atone for something. In fact, the hidden psychological factor in gambling is that people will stand to lose, but they won't stand to win. I know that sounds strange, but the truth is that if they win, they have to go to dinner. But if they lose, they lose all their money; they cash checks until they bounce, they wire their friends for more money, and they keep on losing as though they are dedicated to it. But if they win, they'll stand to win just a minimum amount of money.

Not long ago, I had an experience with a loser. I'm at a racetrack, and a man walks up and says, "Slim, I want to tell my friends that I gambled with you. I'll match you for $100."

I like a little of the edge on any wager I make. So I tell him, "You can lay me $102 to $100, and I'll match you. Otherwise, friend, we'll just have to think of some game of skill."

"What could you think of here?" he asks.

"I tell you what: We'll pitch coins, the closest coin to that wall over there wins."

He agrees, we toss, and I win.

He has a big smile on his face when he hands me the C-note and two singles. "Say, Slim, is it all right if I tell my friends I beat you?"

"Why, hell yes, neighbor—it means nothing to me," I assure him as I pocket the $102 and walk off. There's nothing like a happy loser, I always say.

But the difference between a winner and a loser—and don't you ever forget it!—is a matter of what you think of yourself. I believe that you gamble pretty much the same way that you live your life, that you display in games of chance—although maybe in an exaggerated fashion—the same character traits that make you an individual. In the same way that a writer knows his characters' traits, a smart poker player should know his opponents' moves. A writer friend tells me that if he knows what makes a character tick, he'll know his story plot. And I say if you know your fellow poker player, you'll know his game.

Turn the situation around. It never hurts for potential opponents to think you're more than a little stupid and can hardly count all the money in your hip pocket, much less hold onto it. That's one reason why I wear a big cowboy hat, cowboy boots, and western duds—especially when I'm globe-trotting and looking for high action. People everywhere assume that anyone from Texas in a ten-gallon hat is not only a billionaire but an easy mark, a real hayseed. That's just fine with me, because that's the impression I'm trying to leave. This approach puts those dudes in the category of guessers, and guessers are losers in poker, guessers are losers! That's my meat, to make the other guy guess. If a player makes me a bet, it's me who's guessing whether he's got a hand or not. But if this cat makes me a mediocre bet and I play back at him, he is the one guessing. He's saying to himself, "Well, reckon that slim son of a bitch has got a hand or not?" As a guesser, he's at a psychological disadvantage and getting into a situation where I can move in on him fast.

Of course, no one player continually is going to make the best hand. That's why the ability to bluff, or to sell a hand when you have one, is a major part of strategy. The use of a strong bluff is, of course, less effective in a *limit game* because a wise player who's being bluffed knows that he has a maximum number of bets he can lose and call without being badly hurt. Yet everyone knows *some* player who'll stay in every pot, draw to anything, and play anything, and this type of cat may not risk keeping a bluffer honest, even if his losses weren't very large.

There are many people who think it's clever as hell to check a good hand, then come on strong later. I think that's a pure sucker play. Even so, just about everybody you know who plays poker who isn't a professional thinks that is the cute way to do it: to make a *cinch hand*, check it, and then raise. But I can tell you why it isn't. First, if you check a good hand, another player bets, and then you play back at him, chances are that that player's gone—he had a hand that he'd go broke on anyway.

This very thing happened in a pretournament Hold'em game during the World Series of Poker in Vegas in 1972. I am ribbing Jimmy "the Greek" Snyder to come into a pot. I raise this pot on nothing but nerve; I've got the worst hand you possibly can have: a 7-2.

Jimmy says, "I'd sure come in if I had your hand."

"I tell you what, Jimmy. You call it, and then trade hands with me," I tell him.

He does, and I throw him my cards—a real snowball. Then the flop comes a 7-7-2. The Greek has a full house, sevens full of deuces. He's got a cinch hand; there's no hand out that will beat it.

Jimmy's first action, and damned if he doesn't pass!

The guy next to him bets because he's drawing at a flush. Another player has a pair of deuces in his hand, giving him deuces full of sevens, and he calls the guy shooting for the flush. Jimmy calls, too, pretending to be weak, which if you read the previous chapter, tells you everything you need to know. The next card off, this kid makes his flush.

The Greek checks it again. The flush bets. The guy with the deuces full of sevens raises. It gets back to the Greek, and now he moves all in. As a result, the guy gets rid of his flush and the other man tosses in his full house. The point is this: If the Greek had led off and bet his hand in the beginning, the guy with the flush draw would have raised it, the other full house would have raised it, and all the Greek would have had to do would have been to call the raises. Then these other cats would have got all their chips in, and the Greek would have busted both of them in one pot. As it was, I think he won about $7,000 on that hand that I'd given to him; but if he'd played it right, he'd have won twice that much.

I like to bluff in a high-stakes game and leave it to the other players to guess whether it is real. I don't particularly fancy stud poker, but a few years back I was playing in a stud game. This game is six-handed, and the stakes are high. I'm the only professional sitting in; the other players are businessmen and part-time gamblers. One of the players—I'll call him the Lawyer (he isn't)— is a good friend of mine, but all his life he's had a hankering to beat me out of something. Why, he'd rather take me for $500 than win $2,000 from someone else! When he beats me out of $500, he can tell everybody in town and look like a tree full of owls.

The Lawyer drinks some when he plays—not excessively, but he drinks. (I don't drink. I've got nothing against it, but I believe that the stuff is made to sell. And if I did drink, I'd never drink when I'm playing poker.)

In this game, the Lawyer and I are getting in the same pots. Every time he's in there, I'm in there. Every time I catch an *overcard*, I *lay the lash* to the pot. If the Lawyer's got a 9-7 showing, and I've got a Q-J up, it doesn't make any difference whether I've got a deuce in the hole—I bet higher than hell.

We're playing along, and the Lawyer makes two eights; I have a K-10 up and nothing in the pocket. He leads off and bets those scored eights. I really *play back* at him, which makes him quit those paired eights.

I make sure that he sees my *peewee* hole card as I throw my hand away. He knows I took his money with nothing.

We *rock along*. He pairs tens up. I show a queen-trey. He bets those two tens, and I grab a handful of money and raise him. He can't come up through it; he tosses in the tens. I know that the Lawyer's ass is now getting redder than a trey ball on a pool table. So is his face. He turns purple every time I rake in the pot. Seeing the reaction I'm getting, I think to myself, "The first time that I can get a good hand, I'll cause a spot to be open here."

It's about 4:00 AM, and a big pot comes up between the Lawyer and me. I've got a couple of aces backed up cold turkey. He's got a nine up and another one in the hole. After I fall high with an ace, I lead off with a $50 bet. We're playing fast, anteing $10, which means there's $60 out there at the start. When I bet, another man between us calls and so does the Lawyer; everybody else gets out.

My next card off is a perfect card for me, a deuce. I've got A-2 showing, The other man gets out. The Lawyer has 9-10 up. I bet and he plays back at me. Here's where I use some more poker psychology: I stall and I stall and I stall. I'm thinking, "Uh-huh, this man has got something he's ready to go with." The Lawyer is thinking he has the best hand. I believe that if I'd played back at him right there, he'd have come in the pot anyway. But I only call him.

The next card off to me is a nine spot, which is a good card for me. With his pair of nines, he knows within reason that my nine can't help me much. He's drawn a seven, giving him 7-9-10 up. I have A-2-9 up. But remember, I've got an ace in the hole; so I pass, knowing that I will get this hand paid off.

The Lawyer doesn't want to lose me; he's trying to milk me like a Rocky Mountain goat. He makes kind of a small bet. "Loo-kee here," I think, "he's really got what I thought he had." I know by his actions that he wants to break me in one pot. So I know now is the time to break this boy; however, if I play back at him, he might gnaw loose, although I don't think he will.

Of course, he might two pair out on me there at the tail end. It's possible for anyone in the world to draw out, so I don't jeopardize all my chips. Instead, I just call his bet.

During about the last part of this hand, the Lawyer has called over his little black-and-white pet bulldog, Doc, who sits in his lap while we play. The friendly little bugger seems to be watching the game.

The final card falls perfectly for me—a trey. The Lawyer catches a king. Now I've got these two aces. *He has a pair of nines.* I know that he's either got two nines or two tens, but it doesn't matter, because I've got a *mortal cinch.* There is no need for me to check this pot to the boy, because I know that he's had about enough of me taking his money without having a hand that he's going to sit still for. Yes, he's ripe for picking.

The thing for me to do now is to make it look like a bluff. So I move in on him. Well, he doesn't hesitate too long. He looks down at this little dog on his lap and says playfully, "Doc, you reckon that beanpole has got any kind of hand?"

The bulldog goes "Arf! arf!"

The Lawyer says, "Me neither, I don't think he's got a god-damned thing!" He sweeps all of his chips out there in the pot.

We show our hands.

The Lawyer picks up that bulldog, leaps to his feet, knocking his chair over, and hurls Doc plumb across the room. I felt sorry for that little dog, but he got up and didn't seem to be hurt as he walked off with his head down.

The whole point of this story is this: When you have a mortal lock on a man, there is no need to tell him. If I play back at him early in such a hand, I lose him or there's a possibility that he'll draw out. That is another advantage of the bluff, too: the fewer people you have in a pot, the less chance you are taking on someone drawing out on you. If the Lawyer had moved in on me early, I would have called him because he is an underdog (no pun intended) with what I thought he held. Yet he could have caught himself another nine or a ten or a running pair and won the pot. But the way I played it eliminated any gamble on my part and broke the man.

So I say this—whether you're a friendly game poker player or a *high roller*—when you have a man locked up, there's just no need to tell him. Let him come on in there and when you get ready, you're a cinch to break this person. And if there is a moral to this story, it's this: Never drink when you play poker, and don't ask your dog's opinion on a hand. As I have said before, guessers are losers—even dogs.

ODDS and PERCENTAGES
Figuring the Price of a Hand

$\mathcal{K}$now your prices; that's all it amounts to.

You hear a lot about percentages and odds in the game of poker. Mathematicians, college professors, and expert poker players, based mostly on computer simulations, have written books on this complicated subject. Intricate tables on problematical poker hands are the results. Well, you can play for ten years, and the same two poker hands won't come up against each other again. Possible poker hands in a fifty-two-card deck total 2,598,960.

For myself, I like to keep things as simple as possible when pricing a hand. That way, I can concentrate on the players. For example, when you're in a limit game, the price of a hand is easy to figure. The formula: the amount of money in the pot against the amount of money it's going to cost you, compared to the chances of making your hand. There also is a *hidden percentage* involved, especially in no limit poker, which I'll explain later.

People are always asking me, "Do you ever draw to an inside

straight?" You've heard all of your life that's for the tourists, which ordinarily is true. But there are exceptions to everything.

Suppose that you're playing in a seven-card stud game with a $20 limit. With the last card to come you need an *eight in the belly* to make a straight. Now, if there is not an eight showing, you have four eights in the deck and one draw at it. You also have to look around the table to see how many cards have been exposed, not to mention those in your own hand. So let's say there are forty "unknown" cards in the deck. The odds are 40 to 4 that you won't catch that needed eight. Simple arithmetic will tell you to reduce that fraction to 10 to 1. Let's say that in this $20 limit game there's a $400 pot out there. If all the other players have called and you are last to act, it certainly makes sense to call because the pot is laying you 20 to 1 (your $20 to the $400 in the pot) and the odds are 10 to 1. If there was only $100 in the pot, you would only be getting 5 to 1 on your call and would thus fold your draw with 10 to 1 odds.

Do I ever draw to an inside straight? I'll damn sure draw to one for $20 if there's more than $200 in the pot.

Whether you can figure the price of a hand exactly depends entirely on the game being played and the number of exposed cards. If I can see the cards, I can tell you pretty quickly the exact price on the chances that you'll make your hand. Now, if it's 10 to 1 that you don't make it—and the pot's only laying you 4 to 1— then you're a sucker if you come in. You'd be taking 4 to 1 on a 10 to 1 shot. Turn it around—you want to take 10 to 1 on a 4 to 1 shot.

Another good example of this is a lowball hand. Let's make it *wheel* lowball—ace, deuce, trey, four, and five being the best possible hand. *Player No. 1* stays *pat* with a nine, a seven, an ace, a trey, and a four. *Player No. 2* holds an ace, a deuce, a trey, a six, and a queen. What is the right price for *Player No. 2* to beat what he assumes is a 9-7 pat hand? (No one usually stays pat on a ten.) The only way you can figure these hands, unless you look at all of the discards, is to assume that all of the cards still are in the deck. (Of course, if you have glimpsed a card somewhere because of some clumsy player, you take one card off, naturally.)

Player No. 2 will discard his queen. In order to decide whether he can beat that 9-7, he must figure how many cards that can beat it are out. There are four fours, four fives, and four sevens, making twelve cards that will draw out. There are also four eights and, in this case, four nines. Thus, there are twenty cards in the deck that you can draw that will beat that pat hand.

If these hands were open, the overall figure would be different. You would know that one of your fours, one of your sevens, and one of your nines are gone. By the same token, you'd see that two of your possible losing cards have been eliminated: Either the ace or the trey in his hand would pair you. But the cards are not exposed, so you must figure on twenty winners for you left in the deck. Since ten cards already are gone (five in each hand), that leaves forty-two cards in the deck. You have thrown away your queen, but since you don't know what is in the other man's hand, you must assume you've got twenty winners and twenty-one losers that are out. So a draw to your six against his nine is 21 to 20 that you don't beat the nine. Remember, you are still assuming he *has* a nine. If the game was seven-card lowball and you could see the hands, you could figure it exactly.

The same system is used in draw poker. If you're holding a deuce, a trey, a four, and a five and you're drawing at a straight, you can tell exactly what your price is on drawing that straight. Since you haven't seen the other players' cards, there are four sixes and four aces in the deck that will make your *open-ended straight*. That gives you eight winners, as compared to thirty-four losers, that are out. So it's about 4 to 1 that you don't hit—that's how much the worst of it you've got.

Now, here is where position at the table becomes highly important in figuring your percentages. If you're last to speak and can draw to this hand without a chance of getting raised, then by all means draw, buddy, especially if there are as many as two players who get in the pot ahead of you, because then you'll be getting damn near your proper price. But the main idea, neighbor, is this: If you make this hand, you'll be getting an additional price. This is the concealed percentage in poker that very few people realize, which the mathematicians refer to as *implied odds*. The concealed percentage is not the 4 to 1 odds that you *don't* make it, but what you're going to win if you *do* make it.

Let's say that you're playing no limit draw and two players come in for $200 each (forget the antes in this example), and you shove $200 in there; you're getting laid only 2 to 1 by the pot that you don't make it, which normally wouldn't be good odds at all since you're a 4 to 1 underdog on drawing your straight. But if you do make it and these players have more chips in front of them that you could win, the pot may be laying you as much as 15 to 1 before the betting is over. In other words, let's say you've got $2,000 in chips, and you put in $200 to draw at the straight. If you think you can win the other $1,800 from each of the other players by making your hand, I'd say draw to it. After all, if you don't make it, you can't lose that other $1,800.

Count the money that's in the pot. If there are four players in front of you who have come in, then when you get in, the pot's laying you 4 to 1, and the odds aren't over 4 to 1 that you don't hit your straight. But if you're *under the gun*, that is, the first to play, don't draw at that straight because you don't know whether anyone else will be coming in. You might find yourself against only one player, and that means you're being laid even money by the pot that you won't make your hand. Why in hell take even money on something that's 4 to 1 odds against your winning?

If I say it twenty times in this book it's still not enough: *Never underestimate the importance of position.* In poker, you're at a major advantage when you act last, so you should be playing most of your hands in this position. And just the same, you're at a major disadvantage when you act first, so you should be folding most of your hands in this position.

Or take as an example a six-handed stud poker game. You have a 4-5-6; the pot hasn't been *shot up* too high, and you're trying to trap somebody by drawing at this straight. It's a high price that you will not make it.

Try to remember the exposed cards of the players who have tossed in their hands. But you don't have to remember cards such as the jacks, queens, and kings, because they have no bearing at all on your hand. The key cards for you to keep in mind with your four, five, and six are the deuces and treys and sevens and eights. See if some of these are gone.

Suppose now that the next card that falls for you is a seven. Now you know that you must catch an eight or a trey. So forget about all of those higher cards. We call this a "cut-across," a term that pretty much means you don't have to fret over cards that don't concern your hand.

Assume that there are three players, including yourself, in this pot up until now. You've seen all the up cards; each of you has four cards. That makes twelve. You can't see the other two players' hole cards, but you can bet a horse that they're not treys. They might be eights, but you can bet a new hat that none of them started in there with a trey in the pocket. You have seen three other cards, too—the exposed cards of the three players who dropped out. That makes fifteen cards known to you (you'd better develop a retentive memory, I might add). So you figure this way: "Well, fifteen cards are out of the deck, leaving thirty-seven cards in. Eight of those thirty-seven are winners for me (four eights, four treys). So it is a little better than $3\frac{1}{2}$ to 1 that I don't make my straight."

Okay, now you can see the price that is in the pot. And this is where you are going to trap somebody. Suppose that one player has a couple of queens. He can see that is a cinch against your hand and, in all probability, against the other players' hands, too. Mr. Two-Queens hauls off and makes you a pretty good wager. The second player falls in also. Now, neighbor, come in because they are going to play you for a pair of some kind and not a very high one at that. So if you do catch a stray eight or trey, you are liable to get your hand paid off. Both of the other players have exposed pairs or they are paired anyway, or they wouldn't be betting the way they are.

If you catch a trey, the player with the two queens will lead off betting. You're next, and you'll stall a little as though you were wondering whether to call or not. Since he is a good player, he'll be guessing whether you made a straight. But you have laid the groundwork for this on fourth street—on that fourth card. He is assuming it is 100 to 1 that you started backed up with a scored pair; otherwise, you don't have much business in that pot. So you make Mr. Two-Queens a big bet—one that is really out of line for the pot. If he's a good player, he is going to think, "Uh-huh, he wants me to think he's connected with a straight—he's trying to take my money."

That is what you call playing winning poker. The idea isn't that you're going to make that damn straight, but what's going to happen if you *do* make it. You're liable to cause a vacant chair over there. He may have made two pair, queens up and something. He might have two exposed queens and another one in the hole.

He'll really be trying to sell you a bill of goods, and as a result, you'll break him. Remember, it's not the idea that you're bucking more than $3\frac{1}{2}$ to 1 odds that you *won't* make your straight. It is what will happen if you *do* make that draw.

These are your hidden percentages in poker, especially high-stakes poker.

♠ BASIC ODDS FOR TEXAS HOLD'EM

In Hold'em, figuring odds and percentages doesn't take more than a fourth grader's knowledge of head arithmetic. You'll need to be able to figure out the chances of making your hand after the flop—with two cards to come as well as one card to come.

So let's say you've got a deuce and a four of hearts, and the flop comes 6-10-J, with two hearts. There are nine more hearts out there that will make you a flush. Poker players will say that you have nine *outs*, which is either shorthand for outstanding cards or ways to get *out* of the pot alive, which is essentially the same thing. A shortcut to figure out the price is to multiply your number of outs on the flop by four to get the percentage chance of making your hand. So, with a flush draw on the flop, you have about a 36 percent (9 × 4) chance of improving to a flush by the river (the actual percentage is closer to 35 percent).

Notice that these are the odds of making your hand, and not the odds of missing your hand. To convert percentages to odds, compare the chance of missing to the chance of hitting. In the above example, there is a 65 percent (100 − 35) chance of missing your flush after two more cards. So the odds against hitting the flush with two cards to come are roughly 65 to 35, or about 2 to 1. To figure out the price with one card to come, multiply your number of outs by 2.2—or, if you're lighter than a June frost just multiply by 2 to keep things simple.

Now in this example let's say it's the same flop of six of hearts, ten of spades, and a jack of hearts, and you're holding the ace and king of hearts. If you know your opponent is holding a jack and a deuce of diamonds, he's obviously ahead of you on the flop with one pair. But when you count up your outs—nine hearts, the three other queens that make you a straight, the three remaining aces, and the three remaining kings—you see that you have eighteen outs to beat your opponent. Multiply eighteen by four and you see that you're a huge favorite (72 percent chance) to win this pot, even though your opponent has you beat for the moment and you are technically drawing.

Now let's say a black deuce comes on the turn, giving your opponent two pair. You count your outs now and realize that an ace or a king doesn't help you since you're going to have to make a straight or a flush to beat this player. And if you think that all nine hearts are outs, think again partner! If the deuce of hearts comes, sure you'll make a flush, but your opponent will make a full house. So there are really only eight hearts and the three remaining queens, giving you eleven outs. Multiply eleven by two, and you're about 22 percent to make your hand—about 4 to 1 against.

The thing about percentages is that they *help* you make decisions, but they are only one tool and never really give you anything definite. Let's say there is $100 already in the pot and your opponent bets another $100. Now you are getting 2 to 1 on your call with a price of 4 to 1, so seemingly you should *fold* your hand. But you know what I'll do in this situation?

It depends!

If I'm playing against a real tight player, I might move in on him and he might just throw that two pair in the muck and let me rob him. On the other hand, if my opponent had bet his last $100 and doesn't have any chips in front of him, I would certainly fold. You should know the reason—no implied odds, or, simply put, there's nothing left for me to win if I make my hand. But if he's got a bunch of chips in front of him and I've made a read that he's the type of player who can't lay down a hand (or one who figures me to bluff a lot, which I do), then I'll call. The pot may only be laying me 2 to 1 *now*, but if he's got $1,000 in front of him, it's really laying me 12 to 1.

See how the exact same cards could lead me to three different actions—raise, fold, or call. But without a working knowledge of odds, you can't take things to a higher level. You need to be able to figure out the odds without much thought so you can concentrate on the strategic parts of poker.

Another important concept about odds that you need to remember when you play Hold'em is that when you hold A-K, you will flop a pair about 35 percent of the time. People call A-K "big slick," but those people are usually "big broke." The reason why is that if you're holding A-K, you will *miss* the flop two-thirds of the time. If you're sharper than you look, partner, you should also notice that if your opponent is holding A-K (or A-Q, A-J, K-Q, etc.), he will miss the flop two-thirds of the time.

What you need to take from this is that you can't overvalue this hand, especially in early position. Shoot, if a player has a pair of deuces, he's a small favorite against your A-K. Where this rule really helps is making you understand why a hand like A-J out of position against an aggressive player is such a dog. Since *you* are going to miss the flop two-thirds of the time, you're going to be forced to fold most of the time on the flop. On the other hand, if other players *limp in* before you and you raise from late position, you're going to be able to pick up the pot a lot of the times when you don't make a pair.

Probably less than 5 percent of those who play poker know the proper percentages involved in drawing out on a hand; but if you do some simple, intelligent figuring, you can do some pretty big winning.

HIGH-ACTION DRAW POKER *in* VENEZUELA

I'm on a little business for a casino, on the island of Curaçao, in Netherlands Antilles, which is a rapidly developing resort area that gets big "turista" play, when word comes to me of a rip-snorting high-action draw poker game, jacks or better, in Caracas, Venezuela. (This had to have been more than forty years ago, and even back then, I wasn't a draw poker fan, but I'll play anything and go anywhere in the world if the stakes are high enough.) To get into this Caracas action, I'll need some proper introduction; and a man I know at the casino here says he knows a prominent horse trainer in Caracas who can help me.

They have very good and exciting horse racing there, another sport that I follow and speculate on. I once owned some racehorses myself, but that proved to be a mistake; you should never have a hobby that eats.

It is arranged for me to meet this Caracas horse trainer, so I hop a plane. It isn't very far; I almost could have swam there, since

Curaçao is just off the Venezuelan coast in the West Indies. Arriving in the beautiful capital city, I check into a six-hundred-room resort hotel, as fine a hostelry as you'll ever bed down in.

An appointment is set up with Mr. Romero, who they say is one of the leading horse trainers in this country, where horse training is a highly regarded profession. I can talk easily with people, and Señor Romero and I get along right away. He's a smiling, alert-eyed gentleman with the courteous manners usually found among socially prominent South Americans. He draws on an expensive, long black cigar as we talk, and his dark eyes study me, while I get around to my reason for the visit.

"I'm a professional gambler, Mr. Romero," I say, "and I'm looking for an interesting game. Do you play, sir?"

He chuckles. "It is coincidental that you should ask me, señor. As a matter of fact, I do play at cards, in an exclusive club here in Caracas. The poker is very high—indeed, you might find it lucrative if you are a man of considerable talents." He flashes his pearly white teeth. I give him back his grin. "Well, sir, I'm sure not a cheater, you understand, but I'm a pretty damn good poker player."

He looks just a shade skeptical and studies me in silence. So I put it on. "I imagine everybody in my country thinks of himself as a pretty good player, señor, and they may be, but I *know* goddamn well I am. And when I do business, I do it aboveboard. So I'll be frank with you, Mr. Romero. I'd like to meet the right people and go sit in this high-stake session at your club."

He removes his cigar and gently taps the white ashes into an ashtray, smiling broadly again. "Why, I think that can be arranged, señor."

Then I say something that I think, for a second or two, may be the wrong thing. "I'll give you twenty-five percent of my play, Mr. Romero."

"Oh, no, no, no, señor," He looks up quickly "I am a good player also. I don't want . . ."

"I'll give you twenty-five percent of my play for nothing."

His eyes sparkle. Twenty-five percent for nothing seems mighty enticing to this gentleman.

"I think that will be fine," he says, and we shake hands warmly on it.

We're driven to The Club in his limousine, a long, shiny black, ultrachrome job. A doorman meets us at the ornate entrance, and we walk inside on ankle-deep carpets amid plush furnishings. The Club looks, feels, and smells like money; the sweet smell of prosperity is a smell I enjoy.

I sign my correct name on the guest register—I always sign my legal name wherever I go. That way, after you win, you haven't misrepresented yourself. That keeps down violence, you understand. For example, if you go someplace and you're supposed to be Old So-and-So, an oil-and-gas man from Texas, and then it turns out that you've just got oil on your hair and gas in your stomach— well, there can be poor human relations that follow if you walk away with a bagful.

Mr. Romero, smiling ear to ear and slapping me on the shoulder, introduces me around The Club. I know damn little that's being said because they're speaking Spanish, and just about all I know in Spanish is that *bueno* means "good" and *mejor* is "better."

While I'm meeting all the big shots and the Goody Two-shoes, I'm mentally trying to pick out the poker players. I meet one feller by the name of Gonzales, who, I'm told, owns a chain of resorts around the country. He is a thick-set, impeccably dressed, suave cat, who wears gold-rimmed glasses. His iron-gray hair is getting rather thin. In broken English, Mr. Gonzales tries to impress me with the fact that he's a big man in these parts, but I already know that from his fancy duds, aristocratic bearing, and the fact he's here at this club.

I shake hands with Mr. Alvarez, a local citizen. He doesn't mention what business he's in. He's quiet, nicely tailored, and I'd guess him to be maybe a clothing store or manufacturing executive. Next I'm introduced to a man named Tony (I just don't recall these people's full names). I notice that Tony, who's younger than the others I've met, is a tennis player because of his tennis outfit.

At the club bar, I have a soft drink and meet a different type of dude. His name's Juan, and his looks spell danger: A nasty scar runs from the lobe of his left ear clear around his throat. After we shake hands and Juan glares from beneath bushy brows and smiles just enough so that you can hear his face splintering from the effort, I amble off with Mr. Romero, who, in his fine English, explains that Juan is an "ex–bad boy."

"What do you mean, ex–bad boy?" I ask.

"Well, señor, once they tried to deport him because of his political affiliations, but he controls quite a number of people in this country. He has an unusual nickname—he's known as 'Machete Juan.' But he is a good player in our little games."

Right there, I decide I'll try to beat everybody else before I beat Machete Juan, because he strikes me as the type who takes offense to being a loser in a poker game, and I'm not inclined toward violence.

Before my visit at The Club is over, some of the people I've met invite me to be their guest in the jockey club at the horse races the next day, so another little piece of my work plan falls neatly into place.

When Romero drops me at my hotel, I bring up something that's worrying me. "Romero, I need to know for sure what these people are saying. I don't know enough Spanish to order chili."

"I would be glad to assist you myself, señor, but I will be busy with the horses at the track tomorrow. Perhaps you should employ an interpreter."

"That's a good idea," I tell him as I step out of the limousine. "Why don't you line me up some middle-aged gal, who can dress up right sharp, be seen with me, and help me know what's going on around me."

In that part of the hemisphere you can acquire just about anything you want for a few American dollars, so my Spanish dictionary was easily found. The next morning my room phone rings; and when I answer, a pretty-sounding female voice informs me that she is my interpreter, and will meet me in the coffee shop. Her name is Juanita, and she's a slim, brown-haired, brown-eyed little lady, a lovely woman who speaks excellent English. I explain her duties, and it isn't long before Romero's limousine arrives to take us to the track.

Juanita, who comes from a nice family, fits in immediately as we settle down in the jockey club. I'm wearing my working clothes—an expensive, tailor-made western suit, a pair of $1,000 anteater cowboy boots, and a big $100 Stetson hat, along with a bright shirt and a loud tie. I make my wagers through Juanita. I don't care about betting too much money on the horses, and yet, if you're looking for the kind of money I want to win at poker, you can't be a $2 shooter at the races. You have to advertise. But when my first wager on the horses is $50, I don't have to advertise it—everybody around there knows it. With a $50 bet down there you get a stack of tickets that looks like a bundle of newspapers on the corner. Right off, I lose it all.

But I'm not worried; I know the right people are watching when I place the bets. Pretty soon Mr. Romero comes up to me. "Señor Slim, I have something good in the fourth race. I am running one of my horses in it, but he is sore. My horse could be the favorite, but I do not think he will win." The teeth glisten again.

"What are you trying to suggest, Romero?" I ask.

"Although my horse might be the favorite, there is a horse entered that is nine-to-one odds to win. That horse would be my second choice in the fourth. He will be overlooked a little, at nine to one."

I take my friend's advice and put $200 on old Nine-to-One. They're off, and Romero's horse, sure enough, doesn't run worth a damn. The second-favored horse in the race gets into a little bit of trouble and here comes my horse in.

When they pay off it looks like the national war debt, and I am a big hit in the jockey club. When the waiter brings me a cup of coffee or a soft drink, I tip $5 instead of the usual quarter. I am a sport who wins it and spends it, and that's obvious, I hope.

Between the races, Mr. Gonzales, one of the other club members whom I met the night before, asks me, "Do you play cards as well, señor?"

"Yes, sir! I'm a real good card player, and I've got the canceled checks to prove it." He laughs uproariously at this, and then becomes serious. "At our club after dinner this evening, we will get together and play poker. We would welcome you as our guest at dinner and the game."

"That's mighty neighborly of you, señor. I'll sure as hell be there with bells on."

When the races end, the limousine drops Juanita off at her home and me at the hotel. I don't know how long these cats play in their games, but I like to be fresh in case a session goes on a while. A three-day game is a good tonic for me, and I can play longer if the game is good.

I hit the sack; and when the ringing phone wakes me up, I don't know how long I've been sleeping. I glance at my watch and see that it's 9:30 PM. I've missed dinner at The Club, as planned; but I'll take a little extra sleep over food anytime when I'm getting ready for a game.

The caller is Mr. Gonzales, who wonders if I've had a change of plans. He sounds downright concerned. I make an excuse and apologize and try not to let on that this is exactly the way I wanted things—having them want me out there more than me wanting to be there.

I grab a cab, stop to pick up Juanita, and we arrive at The Club thirty minutes later, where I make a new acquaintance, a light-complexioned, dapper little man who's in the coffee business in Brazil. It's obvious that he carries some weight at The Club; he and Mr. Gonzales seem to be the dominating figures, especially in the poker circle. But, in the back of my mind as we head for the poker table, I know that it's Machete Juan I need on my side.

We draw cards for position, take our seats, and each player is given a stack of chips. I swivel around to my pretty gal interpreter, saying, "Juanita, honey, I need to know how much these chips are worth in money. How much is each color?"

There's some jabbering, after which she tells me: "The white ones are $5 chips, the red ones are $50, and the blue ones are $100." I can see that I've got $1,000 worth of chips. With seven players at the table, that's $7,000.

The players, starting with Gonzales and going clockwise around the table, are Romero, me, Alvarez, Tony the Tennis Player, Machete Juan, and the Coffee Man from Brazil. I don't like to start out bombing people right off when I sit down in a game; I like to leave a good taste with the people I beat, because if you don't, the world gets smaller when you leave them and the places you can return to become fewer. That's what a dear friend meant when he told me one time, "You can shear a sheep many a time, Slim, but you can skin him only once." Well, I want to shear for a spell. I don't know what kind of players these people are, but I don't really give a damn. My idea is to play the way they play, while we're getting acquainted. I don't know their style of play, or understand their wagering; but I find out that they've got a rule that you can't check a hand and then raise, and while it's an adjustment, that suits me just fine. If I have a hand I'm trying to sell, I'll lead with it, because checking is not worth much anyway.

We get started. There isn't much talk, and I don't know what they're saying when there is, unless I ask Juanita. But I understand a bet and a raise and a check and a pat and a call, since these are part of a universal language in my trade.

It isn't long before my friend Romero loses all the chips he had in front of him. Now, I was waiting for this to happen to somebody, and I wouldn't have cared much even if it had been me. This sounds strange, but I know if I give away this first thousand it's like putting it in the bank. I'll come back the next day and get it, because these dudes don't have to worry about car payments or room rent.

Romero loses his butt drawing at a little straight. He makes it, then gets broke against a flush. I'm deciding he isn't any player at all, this 25 percent silent partner of mine. If I'd had his hand, I might have lost $200 with it, but he loses his whole pile.

This is what I've been waiting to see, though—how much these people will buy after they lose that first thousand. He orders more chips, and I see that most of them are blue: He's bought $2,000 to keep playing. I'm feeling good right now; this is the kind of game I'm after. If a man loses his money, he can get more chips; but, by the same token, I'm wondering about this payoff thing. I haven't seen any money change hands anywhere. I haven't even put any cash on the line yet.

Soon, Romero excuses himself and leaves the table, and I do

the same. In the men's room, I tell Romero, "Tough luck there, friend."

"Yes. Would you have lost that money on that hand, señor?" It's a pride thing with these people, and this is where my human relations program comes in.

"Hell, yes, Romero. There's no way I could've saved my money on that hand."

"That is what I believed. It looked to me as if it was the best hand."

I agree again, and then broach the subject of the payoff. "By the way, neighbor, how do we straighten these chips out when it's over?"

"Everybody is signing for his chips," he tells me.

"I don't recall signing for mine," I say, scratching my head.

He smiles. "That is all right. I have—how is it you say—okayed you, Señor Slim."

"How do you know you can okay me?"

Smilingly, he explains, "Señor, things are commonly known in Caracas, if one is acquainted with the proper people, that is. Over at the hotel where you are staying, I know what you placed in the safe-deposit box." He's congenial as hell about this little bit of information.

I'm some surprised. "Well, who's okaying these other people, Romero?"

"All of them are very honorable men, señor."

"Then I take it you'll okay anything that I win?"

"Oh, yes, anything that you win, you will get, my friend." He claps me on the back again as we return to the table.

The game rocks along. I whisper to sleepy-eyed Juanita, "Honey, the next time that they mention anything involving an element of time, you interrupt and find out what time they quit playing." She nods and seems to doze off again.

But about fifteen minutes later, she comes alive and shoots off a machine-gun string of words. Machete Juan replies with a glower. "He says that he won't stop until the game is over," Juanita tells me. That's something else my ears have been waiting for, though I'd just as soon hear it from someone besides Machete Juan. But it establishes the three main facts I need to know before I can get down to work: I know that it's a good game—by that, I mean a high game; I know I'll get my money if I win; and I know that if some of these cats are going to be losers, I'll get their eyeballs.

At about one in the morning, the waiters and waitresses bring us a snack, and we back up and eat. I visit with Machete Juan because I figure if anybody's going to try to take the best of the game, it will be him.

The hours tick on. The game gets pretty good. Romero loses some more chips, the Coffee Man from Brazil (who's delighted with my coffee-drinking habit) loses about $6,000 (I'm delighted with his losing habit), while Tony the Tennis Player has gone broke a couple of times. So there are plenty of chips on the table.

About 7:00 AM, I can see that none of these cats are used to playing such a long session. Juanita, bless her pretty little shapely body, slumbers peacefully in her chair, since I haven't needed any translating for a while. I'd guess these people usually start their game around 10:00 PM, then break up about 2:00 AM, regardless of who wins or loses. So I know that all this is for my benefit—and, they hope, for their's, too—but it hasn't worked that way. I'm about $7,000 ahead and never have played but one really good pot, where I took $2,000 from the Coffee Man.

A new hand falls around the table. I pick them up—7-10-7-10-10. Not a bad little pat full house.

Gonzales opens, which means he's got jacks or better. *He's holding an ace-high straight—10-J-Q-K-A*. Romero calls the $50 bet. *He's got two kings.* I've been watching Gonzales, and I decide he's prob ably the best player here, besides me, and he's a winner in the game. With these other three players behind me, I see no reason to raise this pot; if Gonzales has two pair or a set of *trips* and I do play back, he's smart enough to get out fast. So I only call the $50.

Next around is Alvarez, who calls. *He's got two pair, fives and sixes.*

Next in line is Tony Tennis. *He's got a flush draw—five, deuce, six, and nine of clubs and the ace of diamonds.* He calls since he's already got a lot in this game. Machete Juan folds, as does the Coffee Man. It's back to Gonzales. He stands pat, and I figure he's probably got a real hand; I've watched him all night and I know what he stays and plays on. He doesn't come in there splashing the water around, and I know he doesn't stay pat on something like two pair and bluff at the pot.

Romero draws three cards to his hand. I'm next, and here I sit with this pat full boat. I hesitate slightly, although it must be obvious that I'm probably not standing pat on a bust behind a man who's opened and stood pat. But I'm trying to sell my hand to Gonzales, and I know almost for certain that my pat full is the winning hand.

Alvarez, next behind me, draws one card. Tony also takes one. *Romero catches nothing to improve his two kings. Alvarez has some real bad luck—he catches a six that makes him sixes full of fives. And the ace of clubs hits Tony, which gives him an ace-high flush.*

The next betting interval, Gonzales leads off and bets $300, which makes me wonder what this boy's holding, since I'm behind him and standing pat. He's figuring me for either a busted hand—cold bluff or a small straight; because if I'm pat with a full house or a flush or a set of fours, his hand is no good. Romero throws his hand in.

It's to me now and I'm thinking about raising it. But there are two people behind me, each who drew only one card. They're either drawing to a straight, a flush, or two pair. So I have no reason to play back at Gonzales at this point, because I'm hoping that one of these guys behind me made his hand. And that he was drawing to a big hand and that he'll bump it. I just call the $300.

Sure enough, Mr. Alvarez, *who made his sixes full of fives*, plays back at Gonzales, and raises the pot $800. Then it comes to Tony Tennis, who knows that Gonzales stood pat, that Alvarez drew only one, and I stood pat. He probably thinks that if Gonzales and I stood pat with a flush or a straight, his ace-high flush is the best hand. Tony calls the $1,100 and shoves in $700 more, all of his chips. When it gets back to Gonzales, he has to come in with his ace-high straight. He calls with the rest of his chips.

Now is the time for me to play my full house, but the only player with any money left is Alvarez. *Fortunately, he's got the second-best hand out.* I move in. He stalls at my big bet and gets to thinking. I know what he's thinking about: that I can't afford to play back at him like that with a straight or a flush—I've got to have a bigger hand than that. This pot has gotten *out of shape*, neighbor; and it got that way because of the way I played my hand before the draw. Alvarez calls his last money off, and I break four players in this one pot. It gets real quiet now, because there was real money in that pot. Tony Tennis had the least amount in it, and hell, he'd contributed over $1,700.

We play on for another hour, and the game ends—at their preference, not mine.

Fortunately, Machete Juan, who's a tight player, didn't lose too much money. I still was trying to show a little favoritism to that cat. But after a parting glower, he was gone. The Coffee Man lost a bundle, but it didn't seem to bother him at all.

I won that last big pot that cleaned out four players because I played winning poker. I didn't play back before the draw with that full house. If I had, maybe I'd have won one more bet from Gonzales, because he's no fool at cards. He just would have called, surely no more, and the next time around he'd have checked that straight real fast. When you hold a big hand and are *up front*, don't scare out the people who are drawing. They may draw and do something that isn't good for them, like Alvarez and Tony did.

With the game at an end, there's some excitement among the small knot of hangers-on, waiters, bartenders, and the like. They crowd around, and it wakes Juanita up. I'm sure she's been pulling for me to win, because she knows her salary probably will double if I have a good night. Her wages for the night were supposed to be $12. I don't think she had to interpret more than fifteen times during the night; but much to that pretty little gal's surprise, she gets two $100 bills from me, just for helping me out. Her eyes shine like stars in a South American summer sky.

I played one more time with these same players, and the game never did get out of shape. Then I heard that the Coffee Man would be going to the nearby island of Aruba the next weekend. Just by coincidence, that happened to be exactly where I was going, and we played some more cards.

I could bore you to death with strategy and theory, but I'm hoping that you can hear a story like this and learn a little something. From knowing how to act in a new game to reading your players to disguising a hand, there are many lessons from this experience that I hope you can turn into profitable situations.

DRAW POKER, JACKS or BETTER

*F*ive-card draw poker is somewhat out of style nowadays. Still, I'm sure it remains a popular game in some circles, especially the family games where Granddaddy taught draw to Daddy and Daddy taught it to Sonny and it comes down through the generations like a family heirloom. Originally, of course, draw was *the* poker game, even with the professionals, but over the years it tended to lose its excitement.

I don't like draw because it's a game in which you must tattle-tale your hand: It doesn't take any wizard to know that when you open, you've got to have jacks or better—that's the name of the game. I played quite a bit of draw when I first started playing poker seriously; and I've won some bundles with it, as I did in that big game in Caracas. So here are some pointers for you old draw standbys.

Position and Opening. As in any other poker game, your position at the table (that is, your seat in relation to the location of the dealer) determines what you should hold to open. If I were in any of the first three seats to the left of the dealer in a seven-handed draw poker session, I'd never open on a simple pair of jacks. I'd have to have two aces or better if I were up front. The reason I wouldn't come in with the minimum openers is because anybody that I get any business from has got to have those jacks beat. (I'm referring to strong players who know their game.) Stop and think a minute what happens if you kick off a pot with dead-even openers, two jacks. It comes to the next player or so and he calls you. In all probability, he's drawing at something. But if it gets around to the fifth or sixth player and he raises you, he's saying pretty plainly that he can beat your jacks. He wouldn't be raising unless he could beat you, because by the simple act of opening you've revealed that you have jacks or better, and so he's not in the dark.

So if you open with jacks in the first, second, or third seat, you've got the worst of it unless you help your hand with the draw. After you open, say the fifth player calls and the sixth player really lays some lash to it with a big raise. I don't want any business with him because I know there are only two jacks left in that deck to help my hand, and even if I catch a third jack I might go broke. With only two jacks running wild in there, you have to figure your percentages with the entire deck. If there are seven players, there will be only seventeen cards left for you to draw from. Those two jacks may be in those seventeen cards, or they may be in one of the other players' hands.

So, figuring your price, you know that two jacks are left in forty-seven cards, since the only cards you're supposed to know about are the five you're holding. You've got two cards out of forty-seven cards that'll help your hand. This makes it about 5½ to 1 that you don't catch the jack from one of the three cards that you draw. You can see how much the worst of it you've got.

Jacks at the Far End. It's a different story if you're sitting in the fourth, fifth, sixth, or seventh chair. In these locations, open with two jacks—if someone could've beat 'em they probably would've opened.

It makes a lot more sense to be in one of those last seats and open with a pair of jacks, hoping that you'll catch a running pair or maybe a third jack. And you'll get some business, never fear.

Let's face it, some of the people who play in these weekly games will stay and draw to any combination, whether it's a small straight, a little flush, a pair of fives, or two eights. What's more, they'll draw two cards at these far-fetched possibilities. You're a prohibitive favorite with just your two jacks over anyone that will draw two cards to a straight or a flush or a small pair. That's strictly for the tourists.

Just about everybody in these amateur games does this—draws to a bust—but if you'll avoid this, you'll be a hardship on these people. And that's the idea when you sit down at the table—you're there to win. Even if the other players are your good friends and neighbors, they're your enemies while you play, and there's no such thing as "having mercy." After it's all over, you can help them mow the lawn, or give them their money back, if it makes you feel better.

Aces as Openers. Now, I'll open with two aces anytime. However, if I get a lot of action—say two people call me and the next guy raises—I'll probably *duck* those two aces and throw them away, because I don't know what I'm trying to catch. It's a cinch that the guy who raised could beat two aces; I might even get a third ace and still be beaten by the raiser.

But turn it around: If I'm in that back seat holding two aces and someone in front has opened, I'm going to raise. Here's my reapon. Besides trying to work out my own hand, I'm trying to determine what the opener has. If he's opened with two jacks, two queens, or paired kings, I've certainly got the best hand. Even if he's opened on two small pair, I'm not the underdog that you might think. Why? Because the opener has to guess whether I can already beat what he's holding. By raising big I might win the pot right there without ever drawing to those two aces. Or I might be called, make aces up or three aces, and cause an open seat where the opener's sitting.

Play a Hand Early. I don't believe in legging a hand. You can keep from going broke on a hand if you play it early. Don't wait until after the draw; you can save your money this way.

Say that one player opens with two jacks and I raise, holding two aces, from my position near the back. When it gets around to the field, they all figure on dropping out. If the person who opened has two pair, he'll probably give me the pot; whereas if he's got a straight, he may think that I've got a flush or a full house. Since he's guessing, he might not play back at me, but he should with that straight. I don't think anyone plays well enough to save their money with a pat hand *before* the draw; but you can get loose from a pat hand *after* the draw when you see what the other players are doing. But that's why I tell you to play your hand *before* the draw— you just save money.

I'll show you exactly how you can do this. Suppose one player opens with a concealed straight and I raise him with two aces. When it gets back to him, he moves me in. Well, I'm through with him right there; he's already told me that my two aces aren't any good. (It's now about 60 to 1 that I don't beat that straight, and the pot couldn't possibly be laying 60 to 1 odds. Thus, I've saved my money with that one raise.)

Take another example with these same hands. The opener

stands pat with his straight. I don't raise him, and I draw to my paired aces and catch another ace, a four, and a six. Now I've got to guess whether he's actually got a pat or not, because in draw poker, jacks or better, many a player will stay pat on two pair and bet. Why? Because it's a big gamble that you won't make a full house when you draw anyway. As I've said many times over, the guesser is the loser in poker. In this instance, I'd be guessing whether the opener has a pat or not; and, sure enough, he does. After making those three aces, the average player would go broke with them. I wouldn't, because I'd save my money before the draw by playing back with a big raise and finding out just how strong the opener really is.

Staying on Less Than Openers. Now, if I'm first, second, or third to speak and have a possible straight to draw at, I obviously can't open. Let's suppose, however, that I'm first under the gun and hold a four, a five, a six, and a seven. The next man opens, the following four players call, and then it gets back to me. I'm ready to call it. Unless there's a pat hand out somewhere, I can win if I make my straight.

I know that there isn't a pat hand out; people tell me before the draw what they've got. If one player has a set of threes, for instance, you know he's going to raise and get some chips in there because he can't afford to have all these players drawing and possibly outdrawing his trips. Therefore, since everybody just called, I'll draw at my straight, knowing it'll win if I hit.

When Not to Stay with a Draw. On the other hand, if the player on my left opens, the next two players call, and the following player raises it, then I can't come in with that possible straight for these three reasons: First, if I call that raise, those other players behind me may have limped in with their good hands. So if I put my chips in to draw at this straight, the next player calls it, and the third player moves in and raises the reraiser, my straight probably wouldn't be any good if I made it. (Whenever you put chips in the pot, you've got to think you'll be able to go with your hand.)

Also, I'm out of position; it just reverts to being in poor position, under the gun, first to tattletale your hand. However, if that reraiser raises only a nominal amount, I might call him, because at that time I've got to think my straight will be a winner. Then, too, I'm going to get action from four other players. When that happens, it means the pot is laying me 5 to 1 that I won't make my straight, but the card-draw odds *aren't* 5 to 1 that I won't. I'm talking about a game in which I can bet all my chips, and this is where the hidden percentages come in again. If I make the straight, I can break a player.

Besides, by not being able to open, I don't have a quarter in the pot at this point. There's no reason for me to risk my checks to come in and draw at this "possible." Even if I do come in and make it, I may go broke. So rather than do all this guessing, I know there'll be another deal in about forty seconds and I'll just wait for a new hand.

However, I would play this hand altogether differently in a limit game. I'd go ahead and call this raise and reraise, knowing there is a limit on what I could lose. And if I did make it, I'd sure as hell bet all that I could, because I don't draw to any hand that I won't bet. If you draw at something, make it, and check it, then you're defeating yourself.

Never Pass a "Pat" Hand. Say that I'm in the *No. 3* seat. *Player No. 1* opens this pot, then *No. 2* calls, and I look down and see I'm holding a full house. Now, most players would get pretty excited with this hand and raise it; but that's not the thing to do, as you saw in the previous chapter, where a similar situation came up in that big game in Caracas.

Don't raise with a full house when there are two people in the pot, coming into you. Just even up call, because those two people in front of you can't beat it, or if they could, you'll lose your money anyway if you get a full house beaten. If you do raise at this time, you'll chase out the other players behind you. In this situation, as it arose in the Caracas game, two players behind me were making one-card draws—one to a small full house and the other to a flush. The guy drawing to the small full house raises for you, driving the player with the possible flush and the player with the opening straight right smack into your big full house. That's how the big ones eat up the little ones.

Now, you've probably seen in the movies the fiction where a guy passes a full house. That's a bunch of crap. You *never* pass a full house. You play it, but just limp in there with it, as though you're not really sure of your hand.

By the way, don't immediately yell, "Pat! pat!" when you're staying pat. That's a sure tip-off that *you* are holding a pat hand. Act as if there's some question as to how you'll play the hand— that's the real psychology of poker.

Betting in a Limit Game. Let's talk about limit poker and use the same hands that the players held in the Caracas game. These are the hands.

After the Deal:

Player No. 1, Gonzales, is dealt **10-J-Q-K-A**—ace-high straight.

Player No. 2, Romero, is dealt **K-K-4-9-8**—two kings.

Player No. 3, Amarillo Slim, is dealt **10-10-10-7-7**—full house.

Player No. 4, Alvarez, is dealt **5-5-6-6-9**—two pair.

Player No. 5, Tony, is dealt **2-5-6-9** (clubs), A (diamond)— flush draw.

Player No. 6, Machete Juan, is dealt **Q-5-4-8-3**—a *snowball,* or bust.

Player No. 7, * Coffee Man, is dealt **J-2-8-6-3**—a bust.

Player No. 1 opens—he's got to with his straight. *No. 2* calls with his two kings. Now, when it comes to me, I do exactly the opposite of what I did in the high-stakes game: I immediately *raise* it. Why? Because you must take every opportunity to get some chips in the pot in a game played with a limit, since you can only bet once.

Okay, *No. 4* has fives and sixes, which will cost him two bets (from the opener and me) to come in, but he's aiming for a full house. He calls *No. 5,* who has a flush draw, and he gets in the pot because he already has five bets in ahead of him. *Nos. 6* and 7 fold their bust hands. When it gets back to *No. 1* and his straight, he reraises it.

No. 2, who isn't a very bright player, calls the raise and reraise with his two puny kings because he figures, as many a weak player does, that since he's already this far into the pot, he might as well keep going.

When it gets to me (*No. 3*), I raise again. (This depends, of course, on the raise limit; that is, the number of raises allowed.) *Players No. 4* and 5, with their drawing hands, call my reraise, as does *Player No. 1* when it gets back to him.

*Dealer.

On the draw, *No. 1* stands pat, *No. 2* takes three cards to his two kings and makes a bust, and I (*No. 3*) stand pat, although stalling and trying to sell my hand. *No. 4* draws one card to his pair, making a six full on fives. Player *No. 5* draws one card, getting an ace and making an ace-high (nut) club flush.

Now *No. 1* bets his straight, thinking it's the winning hand, and *Player No. 2*, bless him, finally folds. I (*No. 3*) call the bet and raise, and then *Nos. 4* and *5* also call. Finally, *Player No. 1* calls, ending the betting. And I win a hatful.

So you see, whenever you have a big hand in limit poker, bet on it as hard as you can. It's safe to lay the lash to your hand, because if you run into people with good hands or good draws, they'll stay; they aren't risking all their chips anyway in a limit game. Whether they are weekend or professional players, once they get into a pot, they usually go on with it unless it gets too fast—and it can't do that in a limit game. You'll make more money raising than you will limping a big hand in limit poker.

I've said that you never should pass a full house, but I'll make one exception to that. Occasionally, after the draw in a limit game when it's down to three-handed, you might *sandwich* a player. That doesn't mean you are playing partners with the third guy; but if you're first, you might check it because you know Old So-and-So over there is one of those tight players, and you know goddamn well that he's got a hand when he comes in, because you know what it takes for him to stay. You can figure that if he's in with a good hand, he's probably going to raise it.

♥ SUMMARY POINTS

✦ In five-card draw poker, your position determines what you can open with. In the first three seats, never open with less than two aces.

✦ If you're in seats four, five, six, or seven, you can open with the minimum opener of two jacks, but watch the other hands to see if you should duck these openers after the draw.

✦ If you're holding a big hand, bet and raise at every possible opportunity in a limit game. You've got to build up a pot.

✦ Once players get into a pot, they usually go on unless it gets too fast. However, a strong player knows when to fold a hand.

✦ Never draw at a straight against one player in a limit game.

HOLD'EM

There's a lot of talk about where Texas Hold'em started; some say Corpus Christi, Brenham, or Waco, and some even say Oklahoma or Louisiana, but I'd bet on Texas. I play Hold'em better than any other kind of poker, and, needless to say, I'd rather play it than anything else. I don't think you can find a game more filled with excitement that is also so demanding mentally.

In Hold'em, unless you make a royal flush on the flop, no hand is a mortal cinch to win until that last card falls. In fact, what started as the best hand may end up being the worst because of the many combinations possible.

For some years now Hold'em has been a top game among the high-stakes gamblers of the country; I know, because I've played with all of them—in the East, the West, the North, and the South. The game is also known by other names, including Hold Me and Hold Me, Darling. Today, mainly because of television, No Limit Hold'em is the most popular poker game in America, even at that once-a-week family get-together around the table, because it's a game that can be just as much fun with a nickel ante as a hundred-dollar ante.

It's a simple game to play, but a complex one to master. I'm going to give away a few trade secrets in this chapter, but a word of advice, neighbor: Read this closely and study the examples carefully. Then get a deck of cards and practice; deal out the hands I'm talking about and really get the feel of them. Study the combinations and the possibilities, and then read over the chapter a few more times.

If you can run a bluff, Hold'em is your game, because there is a greater element of bluff in Hold'em than in any other poker game. Lowball, for instance, is not much of a bluffing game, simply because it's hard to misrepresent a hand that's concealed; whereas in Hold'em, five of the seven cards are exposed on the board.

Suppose you've got the ten and jack of diamonds as hole cards. The flop brings the seven of diamonds, the eight of diamonds, and the ten of spades (the community cards, also called the board). Now that doesn't look like much of a hand by usual standards; really, all you've got is two tens. And yet, your hand is a favorite over *two* aces!

Why is your hand—the worst one, obviously—the favorite? Well, neighbor, remember you've got two more cards to come and remember what I taught you earlier about how to figure the odds based on your number of outs. If you catch another ten, you make trips, and there are two tens left in the deck. Other remaining cards that will help your hand are three jacks: You could make jacks and tens, or even three jacks. Four nines are left, which could give you a straight if one falls. There are eight diamonds that could make you a flush (you've got to say eight because you figured the nine of diamonds as a winner in making a straight).

Add up these helping cards—two tens, three jacks, four nines, and eight diamonds—and that's seventeen winners you've got in the deck. With that many winning cards still out, you're damn sure a favorite to beat two aces with that ten, jack of diamonds you're holding.

Now, with you having the ten and jack of diamonds, let's give another player the ace of spades and the ace of clubs. Then suppose that the seven of diamonds, the eight of diamonds, and the ten of spades hit out there in the flop. Your potential draw makes yours the better of the two hands. I'll take your hand and play against those two aces anytime. In twenty hands with these same combinations, I'll win the majority of them. I believe that so strongly that I'll take the 10-J and play freeze-out with anyone and break whoever is playing against me.

I'd even go so far as to say that any tight player with that two-ace hand could turn his cards faceup to me *before the flop* and I'd still call a raise with that ten, jack of diamonds I'm holding. I'm not saying that I'd call a raise with all of my chips, because two aces is the best hand at this point, but I'd call one with up to 10 percent of the chips I have in front of me. The reason here is that hidden percentage I've talked about: If I help my hand, I might be getting laid 10 to 1 odds that I won't win the pot, because this cat with the two aces will go all the way with them. And I'll break him.

But the picture can change drastically with just one card. If the four of clubs, say, was out there instead of that ten of spades, you're no longer holding the best hand. You've eliminated your two tens.

Now you've got twelve outs—nine diamonds and three nines—left in the deck that can make you either a flush or a straight. Otherwise, those last two cards would have to be a 10-10, a 10-J, or a J-J—and the odds of them falling that way are out of this world, roughly in the neighborhood of 150 to 1. So with that four of clubs instead of the ten of spades in the middle, your hand isn't worth anything.

The fourth community card—called the turn—in Hold'em is an important one. This card could make a straight or a flush on the board, or in some other way help a player's hand. It's very unusual if it doesn't help somebody. Just to give an example, say the flop includes a Q-J-5. The fourth up card is dealt and it's a nine. You can bet your horse that somebody in the pot has a ten, giving him a four-card straight draw right there. And if he happens to be holding a K-10 or a 10-8, he's already got himself a straight. Somebody sitting there may have turned three jacks and is feeling good, and suddenly he's looking at a possible straight in another player's hand. That's how much that fourth card can change things.

There are some split pots in Hold'em, because with everybody playing those five community cards, there'll be some equal hands held. This is important for you to realize when you first start playing the game. Watch that board, and if there's a straight there, everybody that stayed in the pot has got a straight. If the flop cards are 7-8-9-10-J, and you're holding a queen, naturally you've got the biggest straight at the table. (You don't use the seven, of course.) You've got the winning hand. If no one has a queen, it's a split pot, and everybody that participated shares in the win. Occasionally, a four-card flush will come up in Hold'em. If there are four hearts on the board and you've got the ace of hearts in your hand, you've got a cinch if the board isn't paired, or if there isn't a possible straight flush out. You'll win with your nut (ace-high) flush.

This is why Hold'em is such a fascinating game. You may come in with an ace of hearts and a trey of diamonds (only if the price was cheap and you were in late position). The flop comes a deuce and four of hearts and a five of clubs. Lookee there, partner, you've got some kind of hand! An even bigger hand would be if the flop included a deuce, four, and five of hearts. With the ace of hearts in your hand, you've got two draws to make a cinch flush. It'd be a cinch flush because it'd be an ace-high flush.

Another example of this is when a player has *pocket* kings in the hole (his two down cards) and the flop brings out the king of diamonds, the seven of clubs, and the eight of hearts. He has to play these three kings because they're a strong hand; but at the same time, this is a dangerous flop in Hold'em.

With no possible straight or flush showing on the board, any fool can see that three kings are the best hand. Then off jumps that fourth community card, a six. With the fall of that six, somebody holding a nine and ten will beat your hand. If a player holds that nine and ten, it's even money that he stayed in for this turn anyway because that seven and eight already on the board is damn near as good a draw as you can get; it gives you all the sixes and all the jacks to make a cinch hand and with two draws at it.

Now, if the player with the three kings leads off and bets, the player with the 9-10 can either play back at him or let it go with a call. But if Mr. Nine-Ten lets it go, he's jeopardizing all of his chips. My own action would be to play back at the player with those three kings because if that man figures to go broke, he'll put some lash to that hand. If Mr. Nine-Ten doesn't play back and that last community card is either a six, a seven, an eight, or a king, Mr. Three-Kings makes a full house and Mr. Nine-Ten has waited until his hand was beaten to go broke with it. A big raise from Mr. Nine-Ten might have run Three-Kings out and won the pot, even without another card.

An important rule to remember: Play your hand fast in Hold'em while you're holding the best cards, unless, of course, you've turned some kind of a mortal cinch like a straight flush with which you can afford to psych some money into the pot. And yet beware of those mortal cinches. If I've got two kings and the flop comes K-7-8, I'm going to make a good bet because with three kings, I'm trapping somebody with a hand like A-K. I'll sure as hell get a call out of him because he's got the biggest card on the board paired, with an ace *kicker*. Or I might catch someone holding the king and eight of spades. After the flop he's got kings and eights, and you can bust this dude; he's going to play those two top pair there on the board.

So I'll have a strong lead with three kings. If I run into a hand and someone plays back at me, I'll call. I've got the top hand, and he's an underdog if he's shooting at a straight. If he's come in with K-7 in his hand, he's *dead to the pot*; if another seven hits, it'll make him seven full of kings, and, by the same token, I'll have kings full of sevens and cause him some misfortune. In Hold'em, you just never know until that final card is turned.

And I'll never forget the time, neighbor, that this was demonstrated to me. I have an expression: "All trappers don't wear fur caps." That came up one time when I beat a feller out of a pot and another player told him, "You let that slim son of a bitch in the cowboy hat take your money," and I told 'em with a grin, "Hell, all trappers don't wear fur caps." But I might have added that sometimes the lambs slaughter the butcher. My thoughts go back to one particular Hold'em game when there were seven of us playing, and we got a good pot started. I'm first action and I don't want to tattletale my hand because I'm sitting behind the best hand possible, pocket aces, or American Airlines as we sometimes like to say.

The flop brings a four, a five, and a seven. The man on my immediate right is Mr. Bill Boyd, an executive at the Golden Nugget Casino in Las Vegas, and, in my opinion, the best stud player in the world. In fact, I'd rather have early frost on my peaches than play stud with Mr. Boyd, but he'll play Hold'em, too. Mr.

Boyd bets. I believe that within reason I can beat whatever he's got. But I don't want to raise him and *stool my hand*, so I just even up call.

Another fellow from Oklahoma City calls it. Also, a dear friend of mine from Tennessee—we call him Long Goody—calls this bet. Now, this boy's a top professional player and good, and I figure him for a hand, which he doesn't tattle on, either. I think the world of Long Goody, although I must say he has been a hardship on me all my life.

The next community card turned is an ace. Well, neighbor, that's practically a cinch hand. I've got a cinch hand unless one of these cats has a six and an eight or a six and a four in the hole. My thinking is that Mr. Boyd probably has himself an ace and another seven, which would make him two pair. If this is so, I'm going to break him.

Sure enough, Bill Boyd bets about $1,600. I figure no need for this slim country boy to run these other folks and their money out, since I know damn well I got the best hand. So once again I just call Mr. Boyd's bet.

Another man around the table passes. It gets to Long Goody, and he raises. Now it's Mr. Boyd's action, and sure enough, he's on a stone-cold bluff and he tosses it in.

But I'm trapping for Goody, and I've got him in my snare. I figure him for trips. *He's got three fives.* So I raise it, and Goody "comes to the center like we did last winter." We get all our chips in the pot, with another card still to come.

"Whatta you got, Slim, you got a hand?" Goody asks.

It doesn't matter what's known now, so I tell him, "Yeah, I got three aces."

He admits he has three fives.

I'm feeling damn good because of the forty-four unknown

cards, there is only one five left that will beat me. It's a 43 to 1 shot that he doesn't get it.

You guessed it, neighbor. The dealer *burned* one and turned one, and off came that five!

It goes to show that losing to a long shot can happen to anyone. That was a case of me trying to trap a man to win all of his money and then having him spring the trap shut on me. (By the way, that boy took those winnings and went home and bought a ranch. With my compliments, I should say, because I sure as hell paid for that spread. He named it the Four-5's Ranch.)

Long Goody is a good player—he used to play in the World Series of Poker every year—and he's done that same thing to me two or three times in my life. Every time that anybody has beat me out of a good pot, I remember it. Like that time during the World Series of Poker in 1970 when we were in another Hold'em game, Long Goody and me.

I have a queen of clubs and a queen of spades as my hole cards. *Long Goody has the queen of diamonds and the eight of diamonds.* The flop consists of the queen of hearts, the six of diamonds, and the four of clubs.

Goody bets and I play back at him. Since I have kind of a reputation as a bluffer, he doesn't think I have a damn thing, so he calls the raise. Now I've really got him tied in this pot. With what he's holding, he's dead to the pot right now; the only thing that could help him would be two diamonds in those last two community cards or a five and a seven, and the odds of that are as slim as my pinkie finger.

It still hurts to think about what happened. The next card off is the seven of diamonds. The last card is the king of diamonds. Goody beat me in another monstrous pot when I held what I thought was a cinch hand.

That boy has *held over* me all his life. That's an expression that can be true in poker—there are players who always seem to make the best hand against you. I hold over certain players myself, one of them is a boy in Louisiana who's a real pro player. Whatever he's got, it never is any good against me.

I've said Hold'em is a game that involves a lot of luck, but it takes some skill, too, if you're going to be a winner. One little trade secret that'll benefit you, though, is to call before the flop, in position, with any two suited cards that are close together. I'm not advising you to stay in any monstrous pot with, say, an ace and a six of diamonds, because there's just one kind of good hand you can make with that—a flush.

But, for instance, if you have the six and seven of diamonds, then stand a raise if there are at least four players in the pot. Why? Because you can make a straight or a flush and bust somebody with that hand. But with that A-6 I spoke of earlier, you can't make a straight; you couldn't with an A-7, an A-8, or an A-9. However, if I've got the ace and four of hearts, I'm coming in for the flop because it might come a deuce and a trey out there, the pot could be checked, and you get a chance to catch a five for free on the next card, making a straight with which you could break somebody. But always remember—and I can't stress this enough—you never have a mortal cinch on a pot until all of the cards are dealt. Let's take another case in point.

Player A has two tens in the hole. The flop on the board is 10-10-2. Now, four tens look like a mortal lock anytime, but in Hold'em, this may not be.

The reason it isn't a cinch even with only two cards to come is because anybody sitting behind *Player A* may have two jacks, two queens, two kings, or two aces in the hole, and they could make four of a kind, ties—any of which would beat *Player A*'s quad tens.

However, if I was one of those players and holding two jacks and the flop comes up 10-10-2, I'd give another player credit for having a ten. Four tens, no. But I'd likely get loose of my hand without losing any big amount of chips. By the same token, if you happen to be *Player A* with those four tens, don't start playing too hard and tattletaling your hand. You've got one of those concealed buggers where you're looking for somebody who's drawing at a flush, or somebody who's come in the pot with a pair of concealed aces, kings, queens, or jacks.

Instead of coming in like a wildcat gusher, check those four tens. If the pot's been raised going in—and it's a cinch that it has—that cat with the two aces won't pay much attention to those two tens on the board. Even if he's thinking somebody has trips, he'll bet his pocket aces. When he does and it gets back to you, just call him—don't reveal your hand yet.

The next card off—it makes no difference what it is—check. You've got no reason to bet at this point. If you do, Mr. Two-Aces is going to think you have one of those tens. But if he bets again— and he will—play back at him now. If he has bet you twice and you've called him both times, he's committed himself to going all the way with this pot. Play back at him and you're going to break that boy. That's trapping with a hand when the trap works for you. You've got that feller in about the same spot as that Texas Aggie coyote that got caught in a trap, chewed three of his legs off, and still was in it.

I want to emphasize the importance of watching the board— the community cards that make up the flop—especially when you first start playing Hold'em. There're some good reasons for this. Since the community cards are played by everyone in the game, it's possible for somebody to hold the same hand that you do—but with a higher kicker. Take this situation, for instance: Two pair is a very common hand in Hold'em. Let's suppose that *Player A* has two sixes in the hole.

The flop comes an eight, an eight, and a deuce. Now *Player A* has sixes and eights. Right now, he's a favorite over an A-K because there are only two more cards to come, and a player with an A-K must catch one of those cards to beat *Player A*'s hand.

The next card off is a ten. *Player A* still holds the best hand. *Player B* has an ace and a king. His hand, then, is two eights, with an ace, a king, and a ten.

The final community card is a ten, and, as a result, *Player A* can't beat anything. *Player B* has tens and eights with an ace kicker. Since only five of the seven cards are played to make a hand, *Player A* has eights and tens with a six kicker. Actually, he's ended up with three pair, which aren't worth a damn. If that last ten hadn't hit, *Player A* would have had a hand, but *Player B*, who didn't have anything to start with, wins that pot on the basis of his ace kicker.

♣ STARTING HANDS IN LIMIT AND NO LIMIT HOLD'EM

Let's pretend that Carl Lewis, when he was in his heyday, challenged you to race him in the hundred-yard dash. For even money, there's no way you'd take that bet. But let's say he offered you 200 to 1 odds. Well, at that price, I might even take it, because he just might pull his hamstring or trip over a pebble. The lesson here, neighbor, is that if you're going to "chase," you better be getting the right price to chase.

You can break starting hands into two categories: strong "made" hands and drawing hands. Big pairs, of course, fall into the first category and suited connectors fall into the second. So if we were playing head-up and you moved *all in* before the flop with your pocket aces, I would certainly fold my 6-7 of clubs. At that point in time, I don't have anything, and the price (even money) isn't right for me to chase. Now, if I've got the same hand and five players limp into the pot in front of me, I know for sure I don't have the best hand, but I'm getting the right price to chase and see if I can make a hand.

When you've got those big pairs, you want to make your opponents pay the price to chase you. That's why you need to raise with them. Otherwise, you'll be giving your opponents the right price to chase, and one of them is likely to draw out on you.

One of the hands that falls in between categories is small pairs. If you've got a pair of fours, you have a made hand and you are a favorite against A-K. So head-up, you want to play this hand fast and make your opponent chase you. But if there are several players in the pot, you really have what amounts to a drawing hand, because two itty-bitty fours don't figure to be enough to win the pot. In reality, you're drawing to make a set, and the odds are about 8 to 1 that another four will come on the flop.

NO LIMIT BEFORE THE FLOP

Small pairs are tricky to play before the flop. If another player raises, it's usually one of two scenarios: Either he's got a bigger pair, in which case you're about a 4 to 1 underdog, or he's got two overcards, and you're only a small favorite. But even in the second instance, you don't know what overcards your opponent has, so if any face card comes up and he bets, you're likely going to have to fold. That's why you either want to play small pairs for cheap when there are a lot of players, or be the one raising in late position so you can play it head-up.

In general, you want to stick to high cards like big pairs, an ace and a king, and two suited face cards. I also don't think you ought to get cute with them. If you get pocket aces or kings, you don't want everyone chasing you, so put in a raise. An exception would be if there are a lot of aggressive players in the game. If you're in early position, sometimes you can just call, wait for them to raise, and then make a bet with some whiskers on it, once they've committed a lot of their chips.

I can't emphasize enough the importance of *position* in any poker game—but especially in No Limit Hold'em. You're at such a disadvantage when you're one of the first players to act that you simply want to fold most of the time when you're in those positions. Under the gun, I've been known to fold a hand as strong as A-Q, because if a player behind me raises, I know I'll be out of position for the next three betting rounds. The other side of that coin is that I have a big advantage when I'm last to act, which is why I'll play more hands in late position and play them real fast. Just remember this rule: tight early, aggressive late.

Perhaps the most important concept before the flop in No Limit Hold'em is that you want to get rid of hands that can be dominated or have potential for second best. A hand like A-Q is worth a raise, but if a tight player raises before it gets to me, I'll toss that A-Q like a hand grenade during an ambush. There's too good of a chance that he's got a pair of aces, kings, or queens, or A-K, in which case he's got me pretty well *locked up*. The same concept is why a hand like A-7 is garbage. If you make a pair of aces, the only one who can give you action is a player who also has an ace—and he's going to have a better kicker than you. This hand has too great a chance of making second best, which is why, with rare exceptions, you don't play it. Even K-Q can be a trap hand and one that you should almost never play for a raise, because too many times you'll be running into A-K or A-Q.

LIMIT BEFORE THE FLOP

The strategy here isn't all that different. You want to play big pairs, high cards, and suited face cards. Position is also important, which is why you'll play tight early and aggressive late.

Limit isn't my game because the power of a bluff is restricted in this game. Because you'll generally have to show down a winner in this game, you can't bully a player and win with sheer aggression. That's why you have to play solid cards and get paid off when you make a hand. If seven players have called before you, there's no sense raising with a hand like A-J. You're not going to get anyone to fold once they've called a bet, and you're not going to be able to buy the pot with a big bet on the flop.

Another major point to keep in mind is that straights and flushes are the strong hands in Hold'em. My theory is that if you make a third of the straights and flushes you draw at in one night, you're going to be a winner in the game. With this in mind, I'll see the flop in No Limit Hold'em for one bet if I'm holding the four and six of hearts, if the pot isn't raised, and I am in late position. I know that if I make a straight or a flush, I'll have a *concealed hand* to trap somebody with. I won't call a big raise with this hand, the four and six of hearts, but I'll call a pretty good-size one if I'm in last position and if as many as three people have come in ahead of me. Then, if the five and seven hits on the board, I've got some kind of hand—4-5-6-7, and two cards to come. If the flop is the ten and eight of hearts and the deuce of spades, I've still got a hand; all the hearts left in the deck will make me a flush.

If the price is right, I'll call before the flop with suited connectors because of the straight and flush possibilities. I'll draw at a flush and take a chance on winning the pot whether I make it or not. My reasoning is this: If I'm drawing at a flush and a player leads off and makes me a bet, I'll usually play back because of my flush draw, which will be a sure hand if I hit. Although I don't have anything at this point—not even a pair—I have a good chance of making my flush. If I play back now and he calls and I *do* make my flush, I damn sure won't have to worry about getting it paid off. The chips will already be in the pot.

But if I just even up call this player and the next card off makes my nut flush, he's going to check his hand, thinking that I might have been drawing at a flush. If I play back at him when he bets and he doesn't call, then I win a pot without even having to draw. If he calls the raise, I'm still not a big underdog, unless he's holding trips; and at the same time, by raising the pot, I'm eliminating the chance of not getting paid off by a good pot if I make my flush.

Salesmanship! That's the name of the game in poker. I'm trying to sell a man a bill of goods when I play back at him. I don't have anything except a draw and guts, but if I make my hand, his chips will be in there and I'll win 'em.

I'm not so strong on doing this with a draw at a straight. For one thing, there's a different price in making a straight than a flush because you have one less out when you're drawing to an open-ended straight. One last word on straights: I don't see any reason for you to lead off and bet on a straight if you make one. As I've said before, you've got a trapping hand—you know you've got a cinch. If somebody takes off after you and there isn't a flush draw on the board, I wouldn't play back at him with this straight. You've already got him, and it doesn't make any difference what hits out there in the middle.

The important thing to do is keep him guessing. That's the nitty-gritty of Hold'em, or any poker game.

OMAHA

O maha is similar to Hold'em in terms of the community cards and the four betting rounds, but each player is dealt four hole cards (instead of two) at the start. The most important difference is that while you can use any of the seven cards in Hold'em to make your hand, in Omaha, you *must* use three of the community cards and two of the cards from your own hand.

Here is where it can get a bit confusing. Let's say the five community cards are A-A-A-K-Q, and your cards are K-J-10-4. If you were playing Hold'em, where you can use any combination of the cards on the board (the community cards) and in your hand, you'd have a full house, with three aces and two kings. But in Omaha, you *must* use three cards from the board and two from your hand. So, in this case, you would use the A-K-Q from the board and the J-10 from your hand to make a straight. You can't use the three aces and the king from the board (that would be four cards) and the one king in your hand to make a full house. So if you were up against a player who had two itty-bitty deuces in his hand, he would have you beat.

I happen to like Omaha. It can be played for high only or for hi-lo split, and for some reason, it seems like when it is played high only, it is played pot limit, and when it is played hi-lo split, it's played with a limit.

While it's a game of people and bluffing like Hold'em, it's also a game of patience. Because of all the combinations out there, you're usually going to have to make the nut hand to win the pot. In fact, if there's a pair on the board, your straight or flush is as useful as teets on a boar, since someone will almost always have a full house. And when you're playing hi-lo, you'll usually need the nut low to take that side of a pot. Now this doesn't mean you need to be a locksmith and wait only for nut hands, because there are opportunities to bluff, especially against overly cautious opponents, but you better beware of putting a lot of money into the pot with a second-best hand.

Now let's start with hi-lo split for some specific strategy.

♦ OMAHA HI-LO SPLIT (OMAHA 8)

Even though hi-lo indicates that the high hand gets half the pot, it doesn't always work that way. The game has evolved so that there is a "qualifier" for low. In order to have a low hand, you must have five cards that are an eight or lower to make a low hand. That's why the game is referred to as "Omaha eight or better," or just "Omaha 8" for short. So if the flop comes 10-J-Q, there will not be a low hand, and the high hand will get the entire pot. If it comes 8-10-J, there could still be a low if the next two cards are lower than an eight. But the smart players won't chase that low, and the bad ones will, which is one of the many reasons this game can be profitable.

So while there are occasions where the pot odds justify playing for just the high or just the low, Omaha 8 is about scooping the pot—or *hogging* it, as we say in Texas. Many bad players focus on hands with A-2 or A-3 that make the nut low. But partner, what you want to do is make that nut low and also make a straight or a flush to go with it. Or better yet, make that full house and have the other players *drawing* to a low, only for that third low card never to hit the board so you hog it all.

The most fundamental advice I can give you for this game is to *fit or fold*. That's right, fit or fold. If the flop doesn't fit your hand, get the hell out of the pot. If your hand is A-2-3-4 with suited diamonds and hearts, that's a great hand to play before the flop. But if the flop comes the 9-10-J of spades, you can't possibly make a low or a flush, and it's time for you to say sayonara. So no matter how good your hand looks before the flop, don't get married to it. If the flop doesn't *fit*, *fold* and wait for the times that it does.

The best thing for you to do to get the hang of Omaha 8 is to deal out five community cards and get used to figuring out what the nut hands are. For example:

A-3-5-9-J of different suits:	2-4 for low; 4-6 for a straight
A-2-3-10-J of different suits:	4-5 for low; K-Q for a straight
7-8-9-10-J of different suits:	*no low*; K-Q for a straight
2-2-3-4-10 of different suits:	A-5 for low; four 2s for high (10s full would be the second-best high hand)

Now let's look at this last hand. The nut low is A-5. The second nut low is A-6 and the third nut low is 5-6. You'll get the hang of it after a while. Just remember that you can only use three cards from the board and two from your hand.

While Hold'em is a game that favors the aggressor, Omaha 8 is a game of both *push* and *pull*. Let's say that after the cards have been dealt, there are six players in the pot, and you are second to act. The board is 4-7-8-9-J, and you have A-2-10-10. The first thing you should notice is that you do *not* have a straight. Since you have to use two from your hand, you can't just plug in that ten from your hand to go with the four cards on the board. What you do have is the nut low with your A-2, but nothing more than a pair of tens for high.

If the first player to act bets, you might be inclined to raise since you have the nut low. But, partner, that's the last thing you'd want to do! Since you can only win half the pot and you've got the nut hand for low, you want everyone to call. You want the player with the A-3 to think his low is good, and you want all the high hands calling for their half. This is an example when you want to *pull* and not push. Just go ahead and call it and hope everyone else does, too.

Another thing you have to worry about—and this comes up more than you might think—is that another player also may have A-2, in which case you would only get a quarter of the pot. Shoot, I've seen it where four people have A-2, and you end up with an eighth of the pot.

Now in this same scenario, if there were six players and you were last to act, and all five players were in, you'd put a raise in with that A-2. Even if two other players have A-2, you're still going to get one-sixth of the pot and break even, and if everyone is just calling, you might be the only A-2.

Reading players in Omaha is key, and it can be hard because every player has four cards. Let's say you've read old Billy as the type of player who *only* raises before the flop with low hands, and sure enough, he raises. You're on the big blind with K-K-Q-J and are certainly going to call one more bet with this hand. Now the flop comes 9-9-5. You figure there's no way he's got a nine in his hand and that your kings up have to be good. The problem is that it's possible that Billy has a hand like A-2-3-9 and could have you beat with trips. That's just one of those things about Omaha that you have to adjust to.

But even with those types of scenarios, if you're a sharp player, you'll still be able to get a read on your players and know sometimes if they're going for high or low. Suppose the flop is 9-8-4 of different suits and a real tight player bets in front of you. You're holding 7-10-J-A, which gives you a *wraparound straight draw*. Any six, seven, ten, jack, or queen will give you a straight. You also have a bad low draw with your A-7 that doesn't figure to play into this. You call the bet and an aggressive player behind you is the only other caller.

Now let's say you know the last player is the type who always raised when he's drawing to the nut low or when he flops a set (three of a kind). So when he calls, you figure that he's likely drawing to a straight and/or has a low draw that isn't the nuts.

The turn card brings a king, and the tight player bets again. Well, you know that he almost certainly has a set, so you just call, hoping to make your straight. The aggressive player behind you just calls as well.

The river is a three, so the board is now 9-8-4-K-3. You missed your straight, but you have A-7, a bad low. You also see that there isn't a possible straight or flush out there. The first player bets again, and now you have a decision to make. Sure, he could have a set and still have a better low than you, if he had a hand like 9-9-A-2, but if you're confident that two of his cards are nines, it's unlikely. Keep in mind that there are five low hands that beat you: A-2, A-5, A-6, 2-5, and 2-6. Well, since there's a pretty good chance the last player has one of those hands (and you're all but certain that he doesn't have A-2), here is a situation where you might raise!

If he's a thinking player (and remember that those are the ones you can make a move on—a player who doesn't think can't be fooled because he just calls mindlessly), he'll read you for A-2, read the first player for a set, and realize that it's not worth it to call two bets to win half the pot, even with a hand like A-5. Now, that's surely an expert play and only one you can make if you know your players and have a lot of experience, but it also goes to show that there is a lot of strategy in Omaha, and it requires a heck of a lot more than waiting for the nuts to win.

♠ STARTING HANDS IN OMAHA 8

Before I move on to high only, I do want to give you some guidelines on what hands to start with in this game. If you had a rule to play only hands with an ace or four face cards, you'd stay out of a lot of trouble. A hand like 2-3-9-10, may look good because you can make two different straights and a low hand, but it's an absolutely awful hand that I wouldn't call two cents with. First of all, you need for an ace to show up for you to make the nut low, and even if you can make a straight with your 9-10, you're going to run into problems. If it comes 6-7-8, then you'll have the nut straight, but you'll also be splitting the hand with a player who has A-2 or A-3. And not only do you have to fade a possible full house or flush, but if a nine or a ten hits, there will be a higher straight on board.

Now, you're not going to be dealt A-A-2-3 with both aces suited very often, but this is the type of hand that you're looking for. A-2-K-K, A-2-3-Q, A-K-Q-J, and 10-J-Q-K are solid hands and, of course, become that much better if they are suited. But don't overvalue suited cards without an ace, because if you make a jack-high flush (or even a king-high flush in many cases) in this game, most of the time it's going to be a loser.

And while any hand with A-2 is solid, most players tend to overrate it. First of all, it's hard to make a low, and even if you flop a low draw (J-8-7), you only have four cards to complete your hand. If an ace or a deuce comes, that will pair you and not complete your low. That should make it easy for you to see why A-2-3 is that much stronger. In this same example, any card lower than a six would give you the nut low.

The premium hands that you're looking for are A-A-x-x, A-2-x-x, A-x suited, A-3-x-x, four cards ten or bigger, and K-K with two other cards that go together. Stay close to these guidelines if you're a beginner, and as you get better, you can begin to loosen up a little bit.

If you're going to be a serious Omaha player, you'll need to play thousands of hours and read more about Omaha than is in this chapter. But this should at least give you enough information to win in a game with your friends. If you play only good starting hands, focus on *hogging* the pot, and stick to the rule of *fit or fold*, the odds will be in your favor.

♥ POT LIMIT HIGH OMAHA

I feel like taking the easy way out and telling you to call my fellow Texan Robert Williamson III—who plays the game as well as anyone right now—to teach you the tricks of the trade in this game. Truth is that it has some elements of Omaha 8 as well as some elements of Hold'em.

Like Omaha 8, you want to start with good cards, you want to fit or fold, and you want to make the nuts. But what makes this game so different from limit Omaha 8 is that you can bet the whole pot and run some people off a hand. Because if they know they don't have the nuts—and they won't most of the time—a good-sized bet is often all it takes to steal the pot from them.

You also need to know your odds in this game and use what you know about outs quite often. Let's say you've got the 6-7-10-J, and the flop comes 2-8-9, giving you a "wrap." Any five, six, seven, ten, jack, or queen will make you a straight. Multiply those six cards by four and you have twenty-four outs. But you're not finished counting yet. First, you have to subtract the four cards in your hand, so you're down to twenty. Also see that not all twenty outs give you the nuts. If a ten hits, you'll have a straight with your 7-J, but you'll lose to a player holding J-Q.

Another one of the hidden percentages in Omaha is that you can often determine—based on the betting—that a player will have a certain hand. Let's say, using the same example, that you know that you're up against a set. Well, not only do you have to hit your straight, but you also have to make sure the board doesn't pair, which would give your opponent a full house or four of a kind.

In fact, if I flop that wrap draw, I don't want to put too much money in the pot, because I know I'm going to have to fold if the board pairs on the turn. Instead, I'll try to see the next card for cheap, and if I hit my straight, now I'll put some heat on a player. See, once I make my straight, I now know that a player with a set has exactly ten cards to beat me. If I happen to also have one of the cards on the board, I know he'll have only nine. I also know that it's difficult for all but the best players to fold that set on the turn. Let's say there's $1,000 in the pot, and I'm head-up against a guy who has a set. I'll bet the whole pot, which means he'll be getting 2 to 1 if he calls, when the odds of him hitting that full house are exactly 4 to 1 (with fifty-two cards in the deck, we can subtract the four in his hand, the four in mine, and the four on the board, meaning there are ten out of forty cards to complete his hand).

Now, if you're thinking that *he* has implied odds, you're both right and wrong. You're *right* that he could bet another $3,000 on the river, meaning the pot is really laying him 5 to 1, but you're *wrong* if you think I'm going to call him in that spot.

♣ STARTING HANDS AND POST-FLOP STRATEGY IN POT LIMIT OMAHA

Before you think about starting hands, fast forward one step. Think about what you want to *make* on the flop in this game. Well, I know you want to flop a royal flush or four aces, but let's be real for a second here, neighbor. You want to flop one of three hands—a top set, the nut flush draw, or a big wrap draw.

So if that's what you're hoping to flop, that will tell you what to start with—high pairs, suited aces, and high cards bunched together. A-A-x-x, K-K-x-x, Q-Q-J-10, and A-7-8-9 with the ace suited and the other two cards suited (giving you a chance for a straight flush) are all quality hands. Again, if you're going to play this game for real money, you ought to read a book on this game alone, but that's a start. Of course, as you gain some experience, you can start to play more hands.

Now beyond your pre-flop play, the next most important thing is to fit or fold. If I'm starting to sound like a broken record, then all the better. Again, fit or fold. If you don't flop that top set, nut flush draw, or wrap, get the heck out of the pot.

Well, what about a hand like two pair? Biggest damn trap in the world! Because in Omaha, unlike Hold'em, two pair is almost never enough to win, so you'll need to improve. In other words, you're on a *draw* for four outs—the same as if you've flopped a gutshot straight! And even worse, if the flop comes A-10-4 and you've got A-4, you might have even less than four outs. If another player has a set of tens and a four comes, you're dead meat. And if another player has A-10, your only draw is to a four. So stay the hell away from two pair and send me all the money you save from not playing it!

———

Omaha is probably my second-favorite game and one that any top player should master. For one thing, it's played in so many places now and tends to attract bad players. Also, you'll find that certain cardrooms will have "mixed" games with a round of Hold'em, a round of Omaha, and perhaps a round of stud. In fact, there is an event every year at the World Series of Poker called H.O.S.E. It consists of one round of Hold'em, one round of Omaha 8, one round of high seven-card stud, and one round of hi-lo stud.

FIVE-CARD LOWBALL DRAW

$\mathcal{B}$esides Hold'em, I've played more lowball than any other game, because lowball was very popular with the professional poker players, particularly in California. Stud was the first poker game that gamblers played; and later came draw, jacks or better; but jacks or better got to be a boring game, and the card players sped it up and called it high draw, a game in which you could stand pat with nothing or open with nothing.

That really opened new fields of poker, and I, for one, am glad that it happened because it has benefited the younger players. They can beat the old-timers who are tight players, playing these new games where there's action and so many concealed hands.

When high draw began to fizzle out, players could see that there were many more possible hands to make by playing the worst possible card combinations instead of the best ones, and that's how lowball was born. Lowball caught on fast all over the world. There are three kinds of lowball; which one you play depends largely on where you play it. The three lowball games are:

①   *Wheel lowball.* The best possible hand in this game is ace, deuce, trey, four, five—the wheel, also called a *bicycle* or just a wheel.

②   *Six-four lowball.* Ace, deuce, trey, four, six is the best hand. (The only difference between wheel lowball and six-four lowball is that straights and flushes count against you in six-four and they don't in wheel.)

③   *Deuce-to-seven lowball.* This is the most popular form of lowball played in the South. In this game, the ace is played high, and either a straight or a flush count against you. The best hand in deuce-to-the-seven is deuce, trey, four, five, seven.

There's also a version of lowball called "triple draw" that has become popular in the last couple of years, but since I don't play it much, I'm not qualified to talk about it. But since wheel lowball is being played more frequently than the other types, I will concentrate on it here.

Position Dictates Your Play. Bearing in mind that neither a straight nor a flush count against you in wheel lowball, it's obvious that a draw at a deuce, three, four, five, blank is a million-dollar hand, since the object of the game is to get the lowest possible hand. In lowball, as in any other kind of poker, position is of prime importance when you're deciding how to play your hand. Who acts first and who acts last after the deal makes all the difference.

If you're immediately to the dealer's left, you're the first player to speak. Now anybody who plays poker knows that if you've got a wheel—ace, deuce, trey, four, five—you open with it, and if you get any business, you've got a cinch. But you shouldn't play back (raise with it) before the draw: Let the people around the table draw, so that if they do catch a hand, they can go broke. Don't scare them out right away.

Drawing at a Ten.
If you're holding an ace, deuce, trey, four, ten, naturally you open. What you do with this hand depends on how many players come into the pot; if you happen to get four players, or even three, in the pot, go ahead and draw one card to this ten, because you stand to improve your hand. You can catch, on that draw, a five, a six, a seven, an eight, or a nine. That's twenty winning cards, or almost 40 percent of the deck, in your favor to improve that ten.

If the pot is raised, you should call it and draw one card; you must draw at this stage of the game. So suppose you open with this hand, the next player calls, the feller after him calls, and then the next player raises it. Goddamn, *call* that raise, because you're drawing at what will be a cinch hand if you make it—the wheel. But don't play back at that raise; your hand is no good at this point, before the draw. Yet the toughest you can run into with that raiser will be a pat hand; probably the worst hand that that player could be holding is a ten high with peewees (very small cards), the same as you. And it's natural that he would raise it, trying for a one-card draw at a cinch himself. So don't play back at that raise, just call. You'll get these other two people between you and the raiser in there, too.

Okay, after the draw, let's assume that you catch a nine. The two players following you each take one card and the raiser stands pat. That's a good indication the pat player damn sure has your nine beat, and, even if he doesn't, you can be sure those other two players didn't call a raise to draw at a nine. So watch out for them; you've got no reason in the world to lead off and bet your nine.

Just pass; and if either of those other players bet, throw your hand away, because it isn't any good, neighbor. I don't care if this *Player No. 2* leads off and bluffs at it, because if the third man passes and that pat player calls *No. 2*, you can figure Mr. Pat for having a hand. If you stop and think, he isn't going to call with a ten, and a ten is all that you can beat with your nine. So duck that hand fast.

Lead with a Seven. But now let's say that in this draw you caught a seven, so you're first. The next two players each take one card and the third guy stays pat. I say you should lead with that seven, because if this cat on your immediate left makes a nine, he isn't going to call you; in fact, even if he makes 8-7, he shouldn't call you.

But if he makes a hellacious hand on his one-card draw, he's got to raise you. Now you're liable to save all your money by having led with your seven and forcing *Player No. 2* to act. Lead with your seven, remembering that you've got an ace, a deuce, a trey, and a four as your other cards—a 7-4 hand. If *No. 2* and *No. 3* pass and this *No. 4* pat hand has a seven, you're going to win his chips. Even if he's got a baby eight, he's going to call you, and by doing that he'll make this hand pay off for you.

Also, by leading off, you won't jeopardize all your chips in a no limit game. After you bet, you guess whether that seven is any good or not. For instance, if the player on your left makes a big bet, the next man passes, and the guy with the pat hand just calls, you know you've got the pat hand beat. If Mr. Pat had something better than your seven, he'd raise instead of call. But hell, there isn't anything but a six or a bicycle under your hand. So lead off with any seven.

Even if you have ace, deuce, trey, six and then catch a seven, go ahead and play it. If it's beaten, you're going to lose anyway, because nobody's so good that he can't play a 7-6 in lowball; and if it's not beaten, you'll get it paid off nicely. That player who stood pat with an eight is not going to bet it after three one-card draws around the table, because if he bets it and gets any business, he knows his hand isn't any good.

If it's down to two-handed—just you and that guy who has the pat hand—and you make a seven, I say really lay some lash to it. This goes for limit or no limit. In no limit, if he can beat your seven, you're going to lose a lot of chips anyway. If he's holding something that can't beat the seven and you lead off and bet him, you'll get a call if he's got an eight or a seven of any description. But if you *check* it, and he's got an 8-7 or something, here's where poker is really played, man. He's got no reason now to bet that 8-7 at you. He'll just show it down; because if he bets that 8-7 and gets called anywhere, his hand isn't any good. Good players don't play 8-7s really fast after the draw (although they do to some extent in two-handed).

Playing a Snowball.

A snow hand, also called a bust, frequently occurs in lowball. So here's an important rule: You never play a snowball from the front position because of the chance of getting raised further around the table. If you get played back at, you've got to duck it and give away that money you've put out there. However, it's a different situation if you're toward the back. If three people come in ahead of you and you're next, now you can call them and play back at them with a snowball. If they've got something like a one-card draw at a nine, they're going to pass. But if they've got a one-card draw at a seven, they'll probably call you, which is all right. The next man, if he's got a pat ten, will probably chuck his hand and give up his money. Meanwhile, the man who is drawing at that seven has 3 to 1 odds against him that he doesn't make it. So I say, always play a snowball from behind.

When that player looking for a seven draws and checks it to you, bet him. I don't care if you're standing pat on two kings and a nine; it doesn't make any difference what your snow is, but, of course, the best snowball to play is a little-bitty one. By that, I mean if you've got two deuces, two fours, and a six in your hand when playing short-handed poker, that's a pretty good lowball hand. Now, everybody says, "Why, that's nothing," and that's the truth; but if you'll stop and think for a minute and do a little mental arithmetic, it's pretty damn hard for that other player to have any little cards with you holding two deuces and two fours and a six. If he comes in and draws one, all the peewees are gone. He's liable to catch a nine, and if he does, he'll check it. That's the time for you to lay the lash to him and make a good, big bet.

Make Any Bluff a Big One.
Anytime you run a bluff, it should be a big one. Don't bluff a piddling amount so that some player will say, "Well, maybe he's got it and maybe he ain't." Lay enough of your chips out there to make him think a long time before he matches them. Then he'll throw that nine away.

Don't Raise and Draw to Anything above an Eight.
That's nothing—it's a tourist play. I don't care if I've got an ace, deuce, trey, nine, that's plainly not a hand when you're in one of those front seats. By the same token, if I've got an ace, deuce, trey, nine, queen, and I'm around toward the back end, with as many as two people coming in ahead of me, I'm coming in because sometimes—contrary to what other experts might say—you've got to draw two cards to play in lowball.

In lowball poker, people say there aren't many two-card draws, and that's the truth. But the reason for that is their position; you can't come in early with a two-card draw because if you get raised a pile of money, you're forfeiting the money you've put into the pot. You either forfeit it, or send the rest of your good money after that which you've already burned up, and I say don't do it. In other words, try to play so that if you come in with something and get it raised, you can come on and protect your money; you can call and draw at your hand. If you miss it, you can save the rest of your chips.

A two-card draw isn't so bad a play. If you do connect, you'll hear people say, "Well, lookee here, he drew two cards and beat this nine for me." Throw your chest out, because it's unusual to beat that nine with a two-card draw. Still, in about one pot out of every five, a two-card draw will do just that—beat a nine.

♦ LOWBALL ACTION IN ALABAMA

Alabama was where the big lowball action was in the sixties, and there was a group of us that used to meet there on occasion for this purpose. In this particular game I'm going to tell you about, people came from all over the country to play. They were all professional players, so it goes without saying that those games generally lasted longer than ordinary games, and there was nothing soft in those kinds of games. You were really looking at the card talent of the world when the poker stakes got this high and those fellers sat down at the table. My reason for being there was that occasionally everybody agreed to change the game from lowball to Hold'em, and when that happened, I immediately became a favorite.

The time I'm speaking of, we're playing seven-handed at a

club—I won't mention the town or the city—but it's in Alabama. It's winter, and cold and damp outside, but not inside the club, where the high action alone could keep things heated up. The game's been going on for a good spell. During the course of play, I've had three seven-hands beaten, which is a hell of a hand to get beaten in lowball, three times no less. This last time, I lose with a 7-6 pat, and all my chips are gone. I start making so many trips to Western Union to renew my bankroll that they know me a block away; after a while, it reaches a point where the Western Union clerk greets me with "Here it is, Mr. Preston." In fact, I've hot-footed it down to Western Union about five times during this game. These guys around the table are really scratching me up.

Among them are such top-notch players as my old friend Johnny Moss from Odessa, Texas, who was the 1970 winner of the World Series of Poker at Las Vegas; and old Long Goody, bless him, the boy from Tennessee who's always causing me some hardship in poker. Goody hangs over my head like that black cloud over that little guy in the *L'il Abner* comic strip, Joe Something-or-Other.

At one point during this Alabama game, I draw at a seven and make it, and another man draws at a seven and makes his, too. I've got a seven, five, four, deuce, ace; while he's got a seven, five, trey, deuce, ace. That four costs me the pot. Damn it, it was one of those hands where if you're beaten, you've got to go broke. Anybody who plays well enough not to go broke with a seven in lowball plays too damn well for me!

I decide then that it's time for me to walk around a little. I'm *slicker than a wet gut* (I've lost all my money), so I decide on getting me some rest. I go to my room and sleep for about six hours; that's what I like to do when I've played a marathon session—not sleep a long period of time right off. I get up and get me some grub and then go sit through a movie, and after that, I return to the room and sleep ten hours more. Yet this doesn't slow the game down at all. There were plenty of players around, and as soon as I got up, someone either took my seat, or else they continued to play six-handed until somebody else joined the action. Feeling just fine after the sleep, I go back to Western Union and get a new bankroll and return to the game.

I'm in a hand and I get a queen, deuce, trey, five, six—a one-card draw at a six-high. I'm in front and I open it, and then it gets around to Long Goody, who's got some sort of hand. Naturally, I don't know what he's got, but he shoots the pot up.

It comes around to the Captain, a grizzled old retired riverboat captain, and he falls in there on top of it. This tells me that the Captain is drawing: I know that with a pat hand, he'd have played back instead of just calling. I've got lots of chips in front of me, so with my deuce, trey, five, six draw, I call Goody's raise. The minute I call him, that ends the betting. Now there are three of us in a pot that a show dog couldn't jump over. I'd won a very big pot just before this hand, and these other boys are also winners in the game, so this game is getting out of shape. This is about the fourth or fifth day that it's been running.

I draw and catch an ace, which is exactly what I was looking for. I look down and see this ace, deuce, trey, five, six, which makes me a 6-5 hand, and I say to myself, "How sweet it is!"

Mr. Goody is no disappointment to me, either; he stands pat. The Captain draws one card, and I figure he's drawing at a seven- or a six-high, or maybe even a wheel. Since I've made my hand, it'll take a wheel or a 6-4 to beat it.

I'm first and I lead off the betting pretty high. Goody stalls and stalls, and I think, "Well, now, this cat's got him a hand." But I don't know whether he's trying to stall the Captain into the pot, or play back at me. However, he disappoints me a little and finally throws in his hand. Then it gets around to the Captain; *he's caught himself an eight-high.* Now, my reputation is such that when the pot gets big enough, I'm liable to bet big whether I've got a hand or not.

Being aware of this, I'm sure that the Captain is thinking, "Well, ol' Slim has caught himself a king, and maybe he's thinking that Goody didn't have a good hand, and that I might pair something." After giving it due consideration, the Captain comes in on top of me. Well, I win a monstrous big pot with that six. A quick glance at my chips (I never count them while I'm playing) shows that for the whole trip now, I'm not in too bad shape, even with those Western Union trots that I've had to make.

We rock along, and about eight or ten hours later, I get jammed into a pot. Somebody has opened it about two seats in front of me, and the next man has called it, and I've got a nine, six, five, deuce, ace—a pat hand. Since there's been no speed shown to this pot, I shoot it up. But now the game's gotten to the point that it's playing sky-high, the way they always do when they run this long.

After I had won this other good pot, Mr. Goody had gone and taken himself a little siesta, and now he's back in his seat. It gets to him and he falls in on top of this, which tells me something: This boy's really a professional player. He knows that two people already have come in this pot, and that I'd raised it. Although those other two players could have a better hand than me, and there's no telling what I've got, Goody still falls in on top of me.

It gets around to the two players who came in ahead of me. The first man calls, and the second raises. I can see now that my 9-6, in all probability, isn't any good. I've got two choices: I can gnaw loose from the damned thing, or I can come on in and draw one card at the six. I decide to call the raise, and so does Goody.

Now the first man, who happens to be Mr. Johnny Moss, raps pat. This is another opportunity for me to remind you of the importance of position. By Johnny acting first, I now know what I have to do. I assume my nine isn't any good, so I discard it and draw a card; Goody also draws one. Damned if I don't catch right back on that nine.

Johnny, who had the pat hand, passes. When he does this after Goody takes one card, I do some quick figuring: There were four of us started in this pot, so I know that's as good as sixteen low cards gone. These other cats sure as hell didn't come in with tens, jacks, queens, kings, or probably even nines, like some damn fools. But there's so much money riding on this pot that after Goody draws his one card, I decide to go with this nine, knowing there aren't many peewees to be drawn at.

If Goody has caught him a nine, he'll probably throw in; even if he catches an eight, he may duck it. I decide to bluff with my nine—although it isn't altogether a bluff. A nine *could* win, but I know it hasn't much chance. I consider it a bluff because if I get called, I know I'm beat.

I move in on Goody, making a big bluff. I reach to the back and pull up some slack and slide to the center. Mr. Goody stalls a while and then throws in his hand. Now I think I'm pretty safe with this nine. I figure that Johnny, the other guy left in the pot, has an 8-7 pat; and if that's so, he's going to throw it away after the bluff I laid on. But Johnny Moss is no ordinary player. That clever old Mr. Moss is sitting there with a fabulous hand. *He is pat with a 6-4!* He trapped me like the pro that he is and broke my skinny country ass.

You see, when I drew my one card, I was drawing dead. Even if I'd caught a trey, which would have been a perfect card for me, or a four, I'd still have had a 6-5 and lost the money.

Well, I felt badly enough about it, and that slicked me off again. I decide that's about the tail end of my playing down here in Alabama, so I get up, put on my overcoat, and head for the door.

Everybody's hollering things like "Slim, are you through? Are you gonna go and leave this money here, or get you some more money and try to win?"

I'm damn sure through with it, though. I tell them, "You can damn sure stick a fork in me because I'm done. I've enjoyed just about as much of this as I can stand."

Johnny Moss and I have been friends for a long time, and he has the courtesy to get up from the table and come talk to me—because he has just won all my money.

He says, kind of worried, "Slim, where you going?"

I already have the door open, and the cold wind was whooshing through, but I turn and tell him, "No one knows where the hobo goes when it snows." And I walk out. That remark has been attributed to me and has stuck all the rest of the years since that game.

Well, it should be obvious to anybody from all that money I lost that Mr. Johnny Moss did the right thing with his hand in that Alabama lowball game. He had a big hand and didn't let on that he had anything, and so I broke myself in that situation. I came off that nine and then came back on it when I drew; and when Johnny checked it, he trapped me.

This is just another damn good example of the benefits of not betting too much with a pat hand before the draw. When you're playing lowball, give everybody a chance to get in and either make a hand that you can beat, or, as in my case, give a fool like me a chance to come in and make something and bluff at it. But start with some kind of hand. This is especially true in limit poker. In any game that's played with a limit, the element of a bluff is practically eliminated, although not completely. If a player shows a lot of weakness to you, then go right ahead and take his chips, if you can, with a bluff. Generally, however, my advice to anyone playing in a limit poker game is don't bluff. You haven't got a dog's chance with a bluff because it only costs a nominal fee to call you.

Most of the so-called experts say that you can't draw two cards playing lowball, but I believe that's old-fashioned. Nowadays, the ante has been graduated in these poker games. If you sit there and wait for a pat hand or for a one-card draw, why, you're apt to have moss all over your seat before you come into a pot. I say that if you've got a solid two-card draw, give it a try now and then. I'm *not* saying draw to an eight, though. If you've got an eight in your hand and still have to draw two cards, you're like that polar bear—you're on a cold-ass trail. You don't have a chance to win with that hand; but say you're holding ace, deuce, trey; ace, deuce, six; or six, five, four. Come in and draw two cards if you're in the tail-end position.

Of course, you've got to realize you've got the worst hand on a two-card draw. Yet if you hit, you're more apt to get the hand paid off, since everyone around the table is snickering, "Well, he drew two cards." And I say you're entitled to win some money off a player if you draw two cards and beat him out.

Your chances of being pat with a good hand are not high in a game. You probably won't hold five pat hands in a twelve-hour session or even in a four-hour get-together. And you probably won't have twenty one-card draws during this same period. So if you're giving up your ante all the time, you'd better try to get some kind of two-card draw and come into some of those pots. You sure as hell can't win anything unless you get in.

One thing is for certain in a lowball limit game: You can't play a snowball—that is, a bust hand. Suppose you have a snow hand, and another player draws one card and catches a ten. He passes, and you try to take his money bluffing with a snowball. By this time, the pot's so big that he's going to come to whatever your limit is on the game; he'll call your one extra bet on the suspicion that you're playing some kind of a snow. So anytime you're tempted to try to run one with a snowball, just remember that old adage of mine, partner: "No one knows where the hobo goes when it snows." And you won't go broke.

FIVE-CARD STUD

$\mathcal{I}$ think stud poker is a game of the past, not only in America but just about anywhere in the world—it's as plain out of style as hoop skirts, ten-cent hamburgers, and passenger trains. There aren't many five-card stud games left in America. In the state of Nevada, good luck finding a game of five-card stud in a casino—and there's also very little stud played in house games. In my opinion, there's just no excitement to five-card stud—it's a dull, lifeless game. I won't play it with the professionals, although I can take care of myself in the average stud game—if I don't go to sleep.

But if you *are* in an area where stud is played, I can give you some pointers that'll make you a winner in those hometown games. I should warn you in advance that I'm not in agreement with the stud strategy that has become practically poker scripture, just because some expert who wrote a book said it was so. Through the years, I've read some of the books that have been written about poker, and I thoroughly disagree with a lot of the authors'

advice on stud poker. Frequently, if you play stud the way some
experts have recommended, you might as well be playing with a
deck of marked cards. Your style will be so obvious that a six-
year-old kid could figure it out.

Everyone knows that the best possible starting hand you can
have in stud is two aces. But if you will not come into a pot unless
you have a ten, a jack, a queen, a king, or an ace in the hole, anybody can play with you for a few hands and know exactly what
you've got. It's more obvious than a marked deck if you are waiting for the big cards to come before you act.

In a ring stud game, if my up card is comparable to the up card
of anyone around the table, and if I've got anything from a seven
on up in the hole, I'll take the next card whether I'm paired or
not. I'm not saying that I'll take a queen and a seven and go after
a player who has an ace up, because I know I've got the worst
of that.

Suppose you've got two fives *back-to-back*. If there isn't another
five showing in any other hand, you've got to assume that the
other two fives are in the deck. If you're playing seven-handed
poker, that means fourteen cards have been dealt, leaving thirty-
eight cards in the deck. In figuring your price, you have two cards
out of thirty-eight to catch in order to make a set of trips. Two
out of thirty-eight would be odds of 18 to 1 that you don't draw
one of those fives.

Why do I believe you should stay and take more than that third
card? As an example, let's say that the third card you draw is a
king. On the next draw, if no fives or kings have appeared on the
board, you've got three kings and the same two fives to help your
hand. By now, twenty-one cards have been dealt, and of the
thirty-one cards left in the deck, five of them are winners for you.
The odds now are only 5 to 1 that you don't catch a five or a king
on that next card.

Now, I don't say that you should take another card if another player has two eights or two tens or any overpair looking at you; but if it is not certain that you're beaten, take another card, because if you catch a five, you're liable to win a monstrous pot. If you catch a king and run into somebody with a pair of aces, why, then you're going to knock some tail feathers out of him with your two pair!

If you're going to stay in the game only on high cards, there is nothing in the world to playing stud, because when you come in you're telling everybody what you've got. If your up card is a deuce and your next card is a seven, all the players know you haven't got a pair of deuces or sevens: You've told them that by your tight playing style. If you happen to catch a queen or a jack and make a bet, then you're telling them, "I've got two queens or two jacks." You *must* diversify your game.

You don't have to have a ten, a jack, a queen, a king, or an ace to come into a pot, although, of course, anybody would love to have those backed-up aces. But you've got to know how to play them, or they won't do you any good, either. If you show too much speed when that second ace lands, you're eliminating any guess as to what you've got in the hole. You sure as hell won't get any business. Unless you run up against a big hand in the first three cards, you can't get those aces paid off. It's like all the other games in this respect—with a good concealed hand, you've got to set a trap for somebody with a betting hand that isn't as good as yours.

An example of this would be if you were backed up with two sixes, and then a third six falls. Another player has an exposed pair of kings. Naturally, the one with the two kings is high, and he bets. He can't afford to check and give you a free card because he figures you might make three sixes on him (which you've already done, of course). Whatever you do, *don't* raise this cat and stool your hand. He's going to bet on those two kings, and you'll win a good pot. You see, if you play back at him when he bets, you're telling him, "Mister, I've got three sixes, so those two kings you've got up are no damn good."

If you've got trips, don't play back at another hand in stud poker. It's goddamn hard to make trips, and you better try to win some money with them while you've got them, instead of running everybody out.

Now, say that same feller has an eight in the hole, and on the next card he catches another eight, while you catch a ten. This man will bet his two kings and eights, and if you play back at him now, he's going to think, "That boy hit his hole card with that ten, so he's got himself tens and sixes. I've made kings and eights. I'm gonna break this man with my two pair." Instead, you can break *him* with your three sixes.

That's the difference between losing and winning poker, neighbor. If you had played back at him with those three sixes at the start, he would have ducked his two kings. Now, instead of winning his one little old bet, you're going to break him, because he won't get loose from those kings and eights, which he thinks will beat your tens and sixes.

So if stud's your thing, keep these points in mind. Your chips will pile up.

SEVEN-CARD STUD

In this game, you're dealt two cards facedown and one card faceup before there's any wagering at all (the rest of the deal consists of three more up cards and one down card), and your first three cards in seven-card stud should determine what you're going to do with the hand.

One of the reasons that I had to become a stud player is that it's my friend Larry Flynt's favorite game. And as you can imagine, when Larry plays, the game has got some whiskers on it. He plays a pretty tough game, and he seems to attract a lot of them Hollywood types—which is why I'll hop on a plane any time I hear he's playing at his Hustler Casino in Los Angeles or wherever else he might be.

While it's not as complex as Hold'em, there is a lot to learn, so let me get right into the nuts and bolts.

Memory is more important in stud than in any other poker game. It's very important in stud to pay attention to the cards that have been played. The best players can remember *every* card that's been played. That's asking a lot, but even if you want to win in a friendly game, you need to at least know which cards are out there that affect *your* hand. If you've got pocket deuces and you see the other two deuces, then chuck that hand since you've got no earthly chance to make trips or four of a kind.

Your hand is *live* if the cards you need to improve it haven't been seen. On the other hand, it's *dead* if they have. If you've got three diamonds and there are five other diamonds showing, get rid of that hand as fast as possible. But if you haven't seen any diamonds, that three-card flush looks awfully promising.

Draw at a Flush. You've got a hand if you're holding three cards of the same suit, especially if all of your cards are live. If the next card makes you a four-card flush draw, then you've got three more cards to make it. Take the full seven-card deal, unless you become convinced that you're up against a full house, in which case you'd be drawing dead. If you're lucky enough to hit this flush on your seventh card, which is concealed, you'll win a bigger pot; but if you've got four diamonds faceup, another player's going to give you credit for having a diamond flush, because you had to have something to start in that pot. So that "down-the-river" card, or "river" for short—that's what the last face-down card is called—is the best possible one on which to make your hand.

However, if the fourth card is of a different suit than that of your first three cards, you don't have any kind of a hand. Of the three cards to come, two must be diamonds for you to win. You're a big underdog, so don't take more than two cards trying to make this flush. If that fourth card doesn't at least give you a pair, and if somebody doesn't make a pretty good wager, why, use your hat for a quirt and whip your ass out of that pot! You have no business in there now.

Draw at a Straight. The same principle holds true if you're shooting at a straight. Let's say you're holding three cards in sequence, maybe 6-7-8. Even if they're all different suits, go ahead and take off another card. However, if you catch something like a deuce to that hand, that should be the end of your drawing; because now you've got a two-card straight draw with just three cards to come, and it's unlikely that you'll be able to improve your hand.

If you're drawing at a three-card straight, it's the same as the flush-draw strategy (again, pay attention to how *live* your cards are): Unless your fourth card helps or pairs you, get out. If the card makes you a pair, then take that fifth card. You may make a set of trips, or two pair, or even the straight you're shooting for. For myself, I'd rather catch that straight card than make a set of trips, because the trips will be wide open for everybody to see, and you can't win a big pot that way. But if that last "down-and-dirty" card makes your straight, the other players are going to be a little hesitant—they'll try to guess whether that card gave you a concealed hand or not.

Incidentally, the odds for your hitting on a straight are damn good if that fourth card is in sequence. Suppose now that you've got 6-7-8-9. With three draws to do it, you can just about bet all your chips that you make the straight, because there are eight cards in the deck that are winners for you—if no fives or tens are exposed on the board. With three draws at the eight cards that would make your straight, don't hesitate about taking the full seven cards to that kind of a draw.

Trips to Start. As everybody knows, if your first three cards are a set of trips—also called being rolled up—then you've got the best possible starting hand in seven-card stud. So by all means, take all seven cards on that hand. It doesn't even matter what your fourth, fifth, and sixth cards are: With four cards still to be dealt, the odds are great that you'll make a full house. Every time you catch a card that's not paired with any of the others showing on the board, there are three more just like it in the deck that will make you a full house. When you draw that last card, you've got ten winners in that deck that'll make you a cinch hand; you've got a shot at a full house or even four of a kind.

Start with a Big Pair.
If you hold any big pair in those first three cards—such as aces, kings, or queens—play aggressively and raise to get other players out of the pot. At this point you probably have the best hand and want to make sure the people drawing pay the price to chase you.

As the hand progresses and you don't improve, and if some cat is obviously making a flush—that is, four faceup cards of the same suit are looking at you—then duck your big pair and wait for another hand.

Play a Small Pair if . . .
Ordinarily, coming into a pot with a small pair is the way you lose your money in seven-card stud and in most other poker games. I'm speaking of anything from eights on down. If I've only got a small pair in those first three cards, I'll see only one more card provided there isn't a raise. If that fourth card doesn't make a set of small trips, I'll duck that hand damned fast; otherwise, I might draw and make it and then go broke. Unless that fourth card two-pairs me or makes trips, I'm through with it.

There is, however, one exception: Suppose you have two eights in the hole and a jack faceup, and your fourth card is a king, a queen, or an ace, and none of your cards are showing anywhere else on the board. In that situation, the deck is what we call *rich* (another way of saying that your hand is live), which means that there's a world of jacks, queens, kings, and aces left in it. In that case, you should take a fifth card.

If you happen to catch an ace, you'll have two pair, and two pair—especially two high pair—is a strong hand in seven-card stud. Now, don't get me wrong: Two pair won't win a real big pot; because if a big pot comes up and the betting gets out of shape, those two pair are strictly for the tourists. The other players wouldn't be in there doing that betting if they couldn't beat them.

Poker is about experience, and there are a million scenarios that can come up when you play seven-card stud, or any game for that matter. The general principles that you've learned apply here. Know your players and watch for tells. Especially in stud, you can get a lot of reactions from players when they are dealt their cards. You can also pick up a lot when they go to look back at their hole cards.

If you're a solid player, you'll know enough to pay attention to see if your cards are live. But if you're an expert, you'll also know if your opponents' cards are live. If I'm able to figure out that Mr. Jones is drawing to a spade flush, I know his chances of making it because I know exactly how many spades are left in the deck. That's a lot of work for some people, but if you want to be an expert, like Chip Reese or Danny Robison (two of the best stud players who ever walked down the turnpike), you need to remember *every* card.

Because there are five betting rounds in seven-card stud, you'll be making more decisions than in any other game. That means you'll have to put all your skills on display. The one thing you can control is what you choose to do after the initial three-card deal.

It's so obvious that I shouldn't have to say it, but whoever *starts* with the best hand usually *finishes* with the best hand. Playing tight and playing aggressive should be enough to make you a winner. Combine that with experience and guts, and you can become an expert.

RAZZ
(Seven-Card Lowball)

Razz, or seven-card lowball, is still a popular game in some places. You'll see it most of the time in "mixed" or "dealer's choice" games, where it will be played for a round or two. We also have a razz tournament every year in the World Series of Poker at Las Vegas. Razz is dealt like seven-card high—two cards down and one card faceup before the first betting interval, followed by three more up cards and one last down card, with betting after each round. And again, as in seven-card high, you should determine from your first three cards how you're going to play the hand. Also, as in five-card lowball, the wheel—ace, deuce, trey, four, five—is the best hand.

With seven cards, don't start with any bad card up. You can play a snowball, or a bust hand, in razz, but if you do (on rare occasions), you want it to be concealed so you can represent a strong hand and bluff at the pot.

Remember to mix up your play, so you won't be a stereotyped player. If you're one of those guys who continually plays only with the *A.B.C.*—that's what we call the ace, deuce, trey—as your starting cards, when you start catching small up cards, you'll look around and find that everybody else is out of the pot. So it's good to play a snow once in a while, even if you lose with it. Of course, don't lose too much with such a hand, but keep them guessing what you'll come in with and what you won't. The guessers are losers, you know.

An eight is a winning hand in seven-card lowball, and yet, while drawing at the eight, you've still got a shot at three lower notches—the seven, the six, and the five. Needless to say, I'd rather have my eight as a down card instead of up so I can represent a stronger hand.

I wouldn't recommend coming in with 6-7-8, although you've got a chance to make that eight and win; with this hand, all you can beat is a nine, and a nine in seven-card low is a bluffing hand and hardly a hand with which to get a heap of chips in the pot. That is, unless you can see that a player's got a couple of picture cards up; then you've got him. So go all the way with that razz hand.

Take another example: If you've got an ace up and a deuce and a king in the hole and you're near the tail-end position, then come in with those cards, because that's a hand that you can misrepresent, since the big king is concealed. However, if that king is up and you come in, you'll get into a world of trouble: If two more people wind up in the pot, even though one may have a worse draw than the other, they can sandwich you. (Sandwiching is when two players get a third guy between them and start raising back and forth to the limit of the raises. They're not actually partners, but they're going to take two to one on their hands by continually seesawing those raises.) Always avoid getting into a spot where you can be sandwiched.

Of course, if you happen to be drawing to an ace, a deuce, a trey, and a four, you're willing to be sandwiched. Yet with just one card to come, you know within reason that you've got the worst of it because those other two players figure to be pat. I'm talking about a situation in which six cards already have been dealt. Of course, the sandwich twins can help their pat hands on that last card, too; if they've got something like 7-5, they've got as much chance at making a bicycle on that last card as you do.

In razz, I don't pay any attention at all to jacks, queens, or kings. It's highly unusual for any of these cards ever to be a winning hand when you show it down. For you to win with one of those damn kings, another player would have to have something as bad as a pair.

Start with a good hand. The only exception to that rule would be if you're playing in a shorthanded game and the ante is big. You don't want to keep running off and leaving your antes, because during the times when you're lucky enough to catch three *babies* (small cards), you'll be the only one in the pot, with no chance at all to get your hand paid off. And the idea in playing poker is not only to make a hand, but to sell it after you make it. Get that hand paid off!

Another concept that you need to apply to razz is the same one you just learned concerning seven-card stud—pay attention to what cards have been played. If you've got 2-3-4-5, you damn well better know how many aces, sixes, sevens, and eights are left in the deck. Especially when you are drawing, you need to know how many of your cards are live to determine the odds of continuing with the hand.

Razz is almost always played with a limit. I have seen only one poker game in my life where there wasn't a limit on razz. This happened at an Elks Club in Texas—probably before you were born.

We played three or four days a week at this club, and usually we played Hold'em, which suited me just fine. Then one day a guy said he was going to deal some seven-card lowball, or razz. Well, I felt I was a little bit of the underdog on this, but I went along anyway. We were playing *table stakes*—no limit on the game.

I catch me an ace, a five, and a six, another man has an ace up, and a third guy has a trey showing; and they bet about $50.

When it gets to me, I bet $3,000.

My reason for doing this is that I'm trying to break up this razz game to start with. I know it's about a dead-even gamble. They've got to have cards identical to mine or have the worst of it. They throw their hands away.

The next time it gets around to me in a hand, I bet all my money on three little cards I'm holding, which wound up this game pretty quickly. That's just an example of why razz is played with a limit. If there's a gambler sitting there, and he starts with three babies, and you've got 6-7-2, he'll bet you all your money. It's still a drawing contest, and the gambler has not necessarily got the best of it with four cards to come. He'd actually be better off waiting until there was just one more card to draw before he bets all his money—but I wouldn't wait.

My idea is that when you've got that other feller beat with the cards you're both holding at the moment, bet all your chips. You're liable to catch a king in the next card to fall, and he may get an eight. Now he's got the best hand, and if he bets all his chips, you're an underdog; whereas with three cards on the table you're a favorite, and with four you become an underdog.

My theory is that you should start with any three cards from the eight on down. If you catch a queen on the fourth card, give up that hand right there. Don't try to catch two little cards out of the next three draws, because you can see the number of people in the pot, and they've got to be holding some of those small cards. So the deck is rich with big cards, and you've got as much chance of catching one of those big ones as they have of getting a little one.

The only situation in which you'd play a bad card in razz is when it's concealed. This is the only time that the element of bluff can be put to use. (That doesn't apply, of course, if you've got a jack up and another man's got a queen showing, because that jack is to the queen the same thing that a seven is to an eight. It seems that's the only reason they put jacks in a deck in lowball—to beat queens.)

Razz, incidentally, sometimes is played with more players than in other games, and this is possible because people continually are dropping out of the pot. I've seen razz games that were nine-handed, and everybody knows that nine times seven is sixty-three; yet they never run out of cards because there are just so many little cards in there that give a player a good staying hand.

Suppose you've got an ace, a deuce, and a nine, and the nine is one of the hole cards. I recommend taking a card to that, but if a bad card falls, quit right there. Don't try to chase the money you've lost starting with that bad card, because you'll only lose more. You're taking the worst of it in trying to make a two-card draw.

If you start with an ace, a deuce, and a concealed nine, then catch a four and get a lot of business, play on because no one is pat at this point. If you make this nine hand the next card off, it figures to be good right away. If you make a 9-6 on that fifth card and some player over there's drawing at a six, he'll call you. But you're still drawing at a six yourself. You've already got a nine made and you're drawing at a six, and, hell, you've got as much right to make your hand as he has. And if neither one of you helps your hand, you win the pot.

Again, like high stud, there are five betting rounds and a million-and-one scenarios that will come up, but the best thing you can do to become a winning razz player is to start with good (low) cards.

THE WILD ONES

ild-card poker games are strictly for the tourists, as far as I'm concerned; high-stakes poker players, the pros, don't play the wild games. I've probably played most of the wild games over the years when sitting in with amateurs, but I always feel as though I'm wasting my time—that the biggest share of these Heinz varieties are for the kiddies. In this chapter, I'll go over some of the more popular games, but if you want a complete run-down on baseball or spit in the ocean or whatever the hell they call these poker distortions, then I suggest you get a copy of Kaptain Kappy's Kiddy Manual.

♠ HI-LO SPLIT

In this variety of poker, the high and the low hands split the pot. This really isn't in the wild-game category because I'll often play

Omaha or seven-card stud hi-lo split for big money. In fact, both of these games are played at the World Series of Poker.

There is one basic secret to winning in this game: almost always go for the low hand, no matter what you hold. It doesn't make any difference if your first cards are three kings; you've got the worst of it in shooting for the high hand in hi-lo split. If someone comes in there and makes just one of those nickel-high straights, or an eight-high straight, or a six-high flush on you, he's going to win both the high and the low.

Again, it's so obvious that it's hardly worth writing: A low hand can become a high hand, but a high hand can't become a low hand. If you're playing hi-lo stud and are dealt 2-3-4, not only could you make a baby straight that could win high and low, but you're also liable to make two pair or three of a kind. But if you're dealt 10-J-Q, you can only make a high straight. If I'm dealt this hand in hi-lo split, I'll look the dealer in the eye and ask him, "Do you speak Spanish?" I don't wait for him to answer before I throw my cards in the middle and say, "Adios."

♥ DR. PEPPER

The wild cards are the tens, twos, and fours—a total of twelve wild cards, or nearly one-fourth of the deck. You must have nearly five of a kind to win, and they have to be awfully damned high. Five of a kind beats a straight flush in Dr. Pepper, and five aces are the best hand.

Since there are so many possible high hands with twelve wild cards, you should stay with only the following combinations: any three wild cards; one wild card and two aces; any two wild cards and three high cards; or a three-card straight flush above a jack (queen, king, ace). Straights, flushes, and full houses aren't worth a damn in this game, so duck them.

I've seen people who'll catch a couple of kings and a deuce and come in the pot, but I don't think that's worth a damn. If I was going to come in with that hand, I'd throw those two kings away and draw four cards to that deuce before I'd draw two cards to three kings. Chances are you'll make a bigger hand than you had.

♣ DEUCES WILD

I guess the most popular wild game is draw poker, deuces wild. In this game, where the four deuces are wild cards, a full house is an overrated hand. You've got no business in a game drawing at a straight or a flush, because if you make either one and get a lot of business, you stand to be beaten. But any time you catch two wild cards in the first five dealt, move in: You've still got two wild cards (deuces) and the possibility of catching pairs to go with the deuces.

Suppose you've got double deuces, a ten, a seven, and an eight. Throw away that ten, seven, and eight (which makes a straight with your wild cards), and draw three cards. Perhaps another person would disagree with this, but I'd rather have those other two wild cards going for me, with the possibility of making a hand bigger than a straight. I think that straights are for the tourists in this game; granted, although at the end of the pot that might be the winning hand, a lot of people will stay pat on that straight, and they'll lose a lot of chips.

Naturally, if it's a straight flush, you don't throw it away. If I had the seven and eight of spades and two wild cards, I'd draw one card to that, because you've got two deuces and a joker that'll make you a straight flush, and you've got the four, five, nine, and ten of spades still in the deck. In other words, you've got an abundance of cards that'll make you a cinch hand.

If you catch a *running pair*, you've already got four of a kind. If you catch anything at all, you're going to make a hand that's as good as your straight, and probably even a higher one than what you started with. So there's no reason to jeopardize your money by staying with a small straight.

When I'm playing deuces wild and see two natural aces, I don't pay any attention to them at all, because they're nothing—that's what the fools sitting there are playing. If you want to be a winner, never come in with a hand like that—having just two aces, with no wild cards or anything else.

Three aces, of course, are a horse of a different color. You've got the other ace plus the four wild cards still in the deck to be drawn at. (You've got to assume those cards are in the deck in any game where you can't see the other hands faceup, because that's the only way you can figure the percentages on your catching them.)

◆ ONE-EYED JACKS, JOKER WILD

Most of the wild-card games are high draw. I play the one-eyed jack just about 50 percent as fast as I play deuces wild because there are only two wild jacks in the deck. That exactly cuts in half the probability of catching a wild card, compared to the four possible wild cards in deuces wild.

Suppose you're holding two fives, a one-eyed jack, a king, and a ten; don't just keep that wild card and draw four. You should take two cards to those two fives and the one-eyed jack. There won't be as many combinations in this game, so you've got a good hand.

♠ SEVEN, TWENTY-SEVEN

Another wild-card game that's played occasionally around the country is seven, twenty-seven. Half the pot goes to the player closest to seven and the other half to the player closest to twenty-seven. To me, however, it's no game at all, because you've either got seven or you've got nothing. In this game, each player is dealt two cards facedown, after which the betting starts. From then on, the cards are all faceup. After two cards are exposed, you can see whether a player has exceeded the seven. All picture cards count as a half, the ace can be played either as one or eleven, and all the other cards count at their numerical value. So if you start with A-6 down, you're sitting on a cinch for half the pot. If you're not exactly on seven, I'd say get rid of the hand, unless you look around the board and see that everyone's up card is a seven or greater, so that you know that the best they could be playing is eight (a player with a seven showing and two face cards in the hole would have eight).

A lot of people who have passed seven will go on and try to make that twenty-seven, but I say that's for the suckers. There's really only one smart way to play this game and that's to start with two small cards. If your first up card puts you over seven, then don't take any more cards—either stay pat, or give up the pot—because if you keep chasing that twenty-seven, you're liable to get scooped for both sides of it; and since the seven and the twenty-seven split the pot, the best you can get would be half the money that's in.

If you're sitting on a seven, don't let on about your hand. When people bet, just call; and if people raise, don't play back—just call—because this is another one of those cases where you've got a cinch. There's no reason to run anybody out who may want to draw. And if there are three people in the pot, you know that you're going to get half of the money from two of them when they go running up that scale, trying for twenty-seven.

But my feeling is that this game is best suited for old women and little kids.

♥ LOW HOLE CARD WILD AND ALL OTHERS LIKE IT

I know of only one game with wild cards that's been played in high-stakes poker by the pros, and that was when some boys from Tennessee thought up a game in which the low hole card and all others like it are wild.

This is a seven-card game. If you have a deuce and a queen in the hole and a deuce up, then you've got two wild cards. However, this is a game that can backfire on you: Always keep in mind that the name of the game is low hole card wild. That final card is dealt facedown. Now, if you start with two fives backed up, you've got two wild cards and what looks like a hell of a hand; but if that seventh card is anything *below* a five, you no longer have those two backed-up wild cards in the hole. Even a backed-up pair of queens is worth nothing, because you have to catch a king on that last card to still have two wild cards—those queens.

One thing is for sure in this game: If you don't have more than one wild card, you haven't got a hand. Let's say you have a six and a queen down and your up card is a jack, and then a seven turns up as your next card. Your six is wild, and all you've got is two queens in that pot. After four cards have been dealt, you can bet a nickel to a dog turd and hold the stakes between your teeth that your hand is no good, because it's a damn cinch that somebody can beat two queens after four cards have been dealt.

Personally, I'd just as soon play old maid as these wild-card games. But the fact remains that if you're playing in home games, you are likely going to be forced to play them, so you better be prepared. The first thing you need to do is adjust and figure out what really is a good hand. The more wild cards, naturally, means that you're going to need a much better hand to win. Also, there's nothing wrong with sitting out a round if a new game comes up. Watch for a round and you'll be that much better prepared to win.

As much as I whine about these games, the truth is that the rules are the same for all the players, so there's still an opportunity to win some money. Be prepared, be ready to adjust, and use your horse sense, and you should come out ahead.

THE WORLD SERIES *of* POKER

Boy, do I miss my old friend from Texas, Benny Binion. For a pudgy old country sonofagun, he might have been the smartest person you've ever met not named Einstein. Benny was also a master of publicity and always seemed to come up with new ways to get people into his casino, Binion's Horseshoe on Fremont Street in downtown Las Vegas.

In 1970, Benny hosted the first World Series of Poker at his casino. He even invited Minnesota Fats and Titanic Thompson, just so the greatest collection of gamblers this country had ever known could be assembled in one place at one time. It's pretty remarkable when you think about it—it was a legendary moment for Las Vegas, and what Benny did forever changed the history of poker in America.

Even though we just did what we always did—which was play poker—Benny called it the World Series of Poker. It got a little bit of publicity, but unlike what Benny had hoped for, it didn't capture the public's attention. Sure, gamblers knew about it, and everyone who stopped by got a kick out of who was there and what was going on, but Benny's plan of attracting the average Joe to poker and putting his casino on the map was a flop.

And here's why: There wasn't any structure to the tournament or anything. All we did was play for a while, and at the end, we all voted on who was the best player. Well, hell, that was kind of a joke, since we all knew that the best player was the one who got the most chips, but we went along with Benny's plan and designated his old buddy Johnny Moss as the first World Series of Poker champion.

But as most things were with Benny, his idea of creating a World Series of Poker wasn't gonna fail even if it killed him, and he got just the break he needed. Ted Thackrey Jr., a feature writer for the *Los Angeles Times*, was there to check out the event. After Johnny Moss was voted the winner, Ted introduced himself to me and said, "You know, Slim, if you all had some way to make this gathering a lot more competitive, it would be an interesting event."

"Competitive!" I said, "How could you be any more competitive than to play for tens of thousands of dollars?"

Here was a man who I didn't know from a grape, and he was questioning me about two things I knew best: gambling and publicity. It wasn't like he was yelling at me or nothing, but when he said, "You got to have a *winner, a real* winner," I shot right back at him and said, "Damn it, we know who the winner is; the person who winds up with all the money."

But he wasn't letting up. "You gotta find some way to make it a contest," Thackrey said. "If you want to get the press involved and turn the World Series into a real sporting event, you need to give it some structure, create some drama, and make it like a real tournament."

"Freeze-out," I said, and brother, that one word changed the face of poker forever.

When Thackrey asked what I meant by that, I explained to him what a freeze-out was—that everyone would just put up a certain amount of money and one guy would get it all.

"That'd get it," Thackrey said.

It got me thinking a little, and it damn sure made a lot of sense. How many people would watch the Kentucky Derby if a bunch of horses ran around the track and then all the jockeys voted on the winner? Or at the baseball World Series, who would give a damn if they just played a bunch of games without any structure and then crowned the world champion based on a ballot? There wasn't any drama in seeing the chips pass back and forth—what got people excited was seeing a person get *eliminated*.

Jack Binion, Benny's oldest son, who might be one of the most powerful gaming executives in the world as I write this in 2005, ran the tournament while Benny kept a low profile and just kinda watched over things, making sure nothing went wrong. Between his reputation and his fondness for keeping a pistol on him, all he had to do was be there to make sure that happened.

Thackrey was right that the freeze-out structure of the tournament was just what the press needed to latch on to the World Series of Poker. There was a pretty good turnout in 1971 (when Moss won again, but this time by eliminating the other players), and by the time the 1972 event rolled around, the press flocked to Vegas like bees after honey to see if Johnny Moss, the Grand Old Man of Poker, could defend his title.

Here I was, back at Binion's Horseshoe for the 1972 World Series of Poker, and in my mind, I had a big old bull's-eye painted on Johnny Moss's forehead. Twelve players had signed up, but four of 'em got so caught up in the side action that they never made the tournament. Then, and now, during the World Series, with poker players from all over the world, there are side games, also called "ring" games, that go on nonstop, and in some of those games, the buy-in can be more than $100,000. It's the greatest smorgasbord in the world for anyone who's ever drawn to a flush, but it's also a great temptation, and some players get broke before the real tournament even starts.

Just like the year before, all the characters were in their places. Jack Binion was running the show, Jimmy the Greek had the microphone, and Benny was telling tales to all the newsmen who Thackrey had set up in a special section. As far as everyone knew, all eight players had put up the $10,000 as their entry fee. But when Thackrey suggested that a big figure like that would make more headlines, Benny decided that for every player who was willing to put in $5,000, he would match that figure and add another $5,000 to the pot. It was just another example of how Benny knew that to make money you had to spend money.

With $80,000 worth of chips, we were roped off on the casino floor of the Horseshoe. Above us, the silent, watchful eye of a camera was there to relay the action to closed-circuit TVs placed all over the casino. Benny, always the marketer, wanted to accommodate the thousands of gamblers who came to watch over the course of what turned out to be a two-day affair. You could hardly breathe in that joint, and the crowd had me more excited than a sore-tailed cat in a room full of rocking chairs.

Of the eight players, five were Texans and three weren't. Aside from myself, the Texans were Johnny Moss, Treetop Strauss, Doyle, and Crandall Addington, a dapper millionaire from San Antonio who changed his entire outfit three times a day. The other three players were Jimmy Casella, a real tough player from New York; a man from Missouri named Roger Van Orsdale, who we all called Jolly Roger; and Walter Clyde Pearson. Pearson was the one who worried me the most. His trademarks were the Cuban cigars that he always chomped on and the flat nose that earned him the nickname Puggy, or just Pug.

Each player started with $10,000 in chips, and the ante started at $10. The minute two players got busted, it went up to $25, then to $50 with four players, and $100 when it got head-up.

To give you an idea of what I was up against, Moss, Doyle, Treetop, and Puggy will probably go down as four of the ten best players who ever lived. And even though I was playing to win, I was also having fun and playing to the crowd. When I pushed all my chips in the pot, the Greek was narrating, and he had the crowd all whooped up. He was droning, "Amarillo Slim's a-movin' in."

"It feels better in!" I yelled, and the crowd cracked up.

Chill Wills, the western actor who grew up with Benny and Johnny down in Dallas, hollered to the crowd, "Who are we rootin' for?" and they yelled back, "Amarillo Slim."

The kibitzers are behind the velvet rope—we call it the rail—and are having the time of their life watching the best players in the world square off against one another. Only the press and the casino executives are allowed in front of the rail. The press boys better be legitimate press, too, because we don't want anybody close to the table who shouldn't be there, for obvious reasons.

Four hours after we begin, gray-haired Jimmy Casella, who yaks about as much as I do while he plays, squints through the smoke-haze of his ever-present cigarette. The flop is a six of clubs, a six of diamonds, and a queen of diamonds in the center. *Jimmy's got the king and ten of diamonds in his hand. Naturally, he's going at a flush, and he's got an overcard, the king.*

Casella leads off and bets. Pug Pearson doesn't raise *although he's got queens full of sixes. He had two queens in the pocket.* Not wanting to stool his hand, he just calls. *He's got the winning hand*—nothing can beat him with the exception of four sixes, and if he's up against four sixes, he's going to go broke anyway holding that full house.

The next card off proves to be a misfortune for Jimmy. It's a four of diamonds. *It makes his flush and seals his doom.* He leads off and bets. Pug calls with no raise, hoping to break this other guy behind him, Jack Strauss, who's as dangerous as a rattlesnake on a rock. But Jack tosses in his hand.

The next card off is a blank. Casella passes, *thinking now that his flush might not be any good.* But Pug moves in on him, and Casella calls with all his chips. That busts him out. This doesn't take anything away from Jimmy's playing, because you might as well be the first man out as the last man out; you came away with the same amount of nothing back then.

The game moves along, and Crandall gets his business in trouble. Crandall is a soft-spoken, likable guy. I'm out of this hand, but I watch it closely. The flop has come a five, a six, and an eight. I'm guessing Crandall's drawing to a straight or a pair. *He's got a 7-8 in his hand, and the flop gives him two eights and an open-ended straight.*

Strauss has a hand, and he and Crandall put in all their chips. *Strauss has two tens in the hole. Now millionaire Crandall's got a million-dollar hand working: There are four fours he can win with, four nines, two eights, and three sevens. He can catch a seven and make two pair—sevens and eights.* The next two cards are blanks, and, in the showdown, Strauss's tens beat Crandall's eights. So two players are out.

With six players remaining, we cash in the $5 chips, drawing high card until someone winds up with $25 worth of the $5 chips. Meanwhile, my good friend Johnny Moss has run his chips up pretty good.

Johnny has two deuces in the pocket. Texas Dolly, as we called my old buddy Doyle, a mammoth-sized gent of 294 pounds back then who didn't look like the cat who won a state track record and was an outstanding college basketball player, leads off. *He has two aces.* Four people call.

The flop comes a two, a seven, and a nine.

Texas Dolly is first to act and he bets. Strauss calls it. *He's got a nine and a jack, which gives him two nines with a jack kicker.* Now it gets to Mr. Moss, who raises it *with his three deuces.* Texas Dolly studies his hand a long time. He probably figures he's going into a concealed hand because it wasn't raised going in. Somebody could have nines and sevens or three nines or three sevens, or he could have what Johnny has (three deuces).

After more deliberation, Texas Dolly says, "Well, if these things aren't any good, I'm ready to get out." So he calls. Strauss folds, knowing his hand is not any good at this point.

Texas Dolly and Moss look through the discards only. Sure enough, there's an ace gone in the eleven cards that are out— counting a burned card and the ten cards of the other five players. So Texas Dolly is dead in the pot unless he gets the remaining ace. The dealer burns one, turns one, and it's a ten; he burns one, turns one, and—it's that *case ace!*

Texas Dolly puts a terrible beat on Johnny Moss.

After that, we rock along, and a hand comes up between Pug, Jolly Roger, and Johnny.

Pug has got two kings in the pocket. He raises it. *Jolly Roger has two nines.* He calls. *Moss also has two nines. This means the hands of Moss and Jolly Roger are dead unless the flop comes a five, a six, a seven, and an eight out there, which would make them straights.* Moss, after losing that big pot to Texas Dolly's drawout, wants action for his last money. So he moves in. Of course, Pug calls it, and when it gets back to Jolly Roger, he calls it. I don't blame him for doing that because now the pot's laying over 3 to 1. They run the cards out, and Pug's two kings win, knocking out both Moss and Jolly Roger. It's pretty unusual to bust two players in one hand.

Pug, Strauss, Texas Dolly, and I are the survivors. I've got the queen and ten of spades. The flop comes the ten of clubs, the four of spades, and the seven of spades.

Now I've got a monstrous hand: Two tens and four spades to draw at, and I'm glad I'm wearing that big-brimmed Stetson of mine. (No one's ever spotted a tell on me that I know of, but a man's eyes show 90 percent of what he's thinking; when I'm wearing my hat, you can only see my eyes when I want you to. Some players wear dark glasses.) With what I'm holding, I wouldn't be much of an underdog if one of these cats has two aces; with two cards to come, I can catch a spade for a flush, or a ten and make trips, or a queen for two pair. Ordinarily, with the ten and queen of spades in the pocket, I'd shoot this pot up, but I've got bad position for a raise.

My bearded friend, Jack Strauss, who seems always to fidget in his chair, limps around in there and catches something. I figure him for two pair. *It was sevens and fours.* But I still think my hand's about equal to his.

Why? Because there are two tens, three queens, and nine spades in there that will make me a hand. So I have fourteen outs with two cards to come.

The turn brings the nine of diamonds. The last community card is an ace, which doesn't help either of us.

So Jack *doubles through* me. His two pair win nearly all my chips. I lose $11,200 in this pot, and that gets me to counting my chips; I usually know what's in front of me, but now I count them anyway. I've got only $1,775 left, with the rest of that $80,000 divided among the other three. I couldn't be much worse off. It takes chips to win at poker.

One of the reporters whom I'd taken a genuine liking to saunters over. He looks damn glum, and leans over, saying, "Slim, a man at the rail is laying twenty-five to one that you don't win it."

"Well, I'm taking $100 of that," I tell him with a grin. I really don't feel like grinning because I realize I've got the worst of that bet. It's a helluva lot higher price than that, as far as the odds on me winning the tournament. I've got to be a 40 to 1 shot with the small pile of chips I've got left. But still, $2,500 to $100 intrigues me, so I latch on to that side wager.

The action moves along without much change.

Then comes a pot and I'm the first in, so I raise it to $100. Texas Dolly calls the $100 and raises another $700. Pug and Strauss both call the $700.

So far, I've got $100 in there and only about $1,700 worth of chips in front of me. I barely glance at one of my cards, noticing that it's a king. I shove back my hat and tell the boys, "Well, there ain't no need for me looking at that other card. I can get action for my money *now*. It makes no difference what that other card is." I push in all my chips.

I'm guessing Texas Dolly's got a fairly high pair. *He has a pair of tens.* Pug and Strauss call my $1,700. The flop comes 5-5-3. Texas Dolly, who's got the lead action, bets $4,000, and Jack and Pug drop out. I'm already all in. Well, I look at my other card and damned if it's not a five of hearts. The trips beat out Texas Dolly's pair of tens.

The $5,200 I win here picks me up; it could be the turning point for me. But I'm still a big underdog; I've got less than $7,000 in chips, and the others have got $73,000 among them.

So we rock on.

The pot's raised $700 by Pug, who doesn't raise very often. He's been trying to sit back and trap with a hand so the rest of us will raise with almost anything, and he'll break somebody with a concealed hand.

Jack calls this raise from Pug. I glance at my hand and see A-K offsuit. Now that's a big hand in Hold'em.

So I lay the lash to it—I shoot this thing way, way up. Texas Dolly's got a snowball; he folds. Pug stalls and stalls. I'm thinking, "I'm gonna run into a hand with this boy."

I always try to determine what my opponent has early in the hand, before the flop. After that, it's a bluffing proposition with me.

Pug finally calls. "Well, lookee here," I think. "Pug's got himself a scored pair—say, sixes, sevens, or eights, huh?" I know that if it's two queens or better, he'll play back at me.

Jack also calls. Then comes the flop: K-3-4. Pug passes. Jack passes.

Since I'm holding A-K, I've got two kings with an ace kicker. I do some quick calculating: If I catch somebody with a K-Q in his hand, I've got him dead to a queen. If I catch somebody with two tens, well, he's dead to a ten hitting.

So I've got what looks to be the winning hand. But that's the fascinating part of this game—its versatility; there are so many concealed hands that can be made. If one of these boys has two treys in the pocket, he'll make trips on me. But I've got a reputation for picking up people's money, so I make a pretty good-sized bet.

Pug calls it.

Jack, who's played with me more than Pug has, thinks I have exactly what I do. He folds. Later, when the hand is over, he tells me exactly what I held, without ever having seen the cards. That's why that boy is so dangerous.

Now I figure Pug for a good hand. *He has a pair of tens.* Pug doesn't think I have a king, so he calls me. Off comes another trey, making me kings and treys, with an ace kicker. That ace is a very important card in my hand for this reason: You must play five cards. If I run into a man with a K-Q, I'm going to win this pot. He'll have kings and treys just like me, but he'll have 'em with a queen kicker.

The next card comes off—a nine spot. I still feel awful good.

Pug checks it.

I bet him $5,000.

He calls.

He loses with tens and treys.

After that hand, it's beginning to be a long night's day. It rocks and rocks along. Now it seems like it's Texas Dolly who's winning all the big pots.

Meanwhile, all of us sitting here except Jack Strauss are hoping that Jack will be knocked out of the game. Understand, it's nothing personal; it's just that Jack is the damn most dangerous Hold'em player—besides me—that there is. He's liable to break you with a deuce and a seven.

Finally, a pot comes up between Texas Dolly and Strauss. Strauss has the best hand, but Texas Dolly's got a good draw. *Jack has a nine and a seven; Texas Dolly's got a nine and a ten.* The flop is 6-7-9. *Texas Dolly's drawing at a straight, and although he's got the worst hand, he can win if an eight hits.* And it does. So far, Texas Dolly has done the best drawing in the game, because Jack is the second player that Texas Dolly's busted out drawing to his hand.

By now, we've been up a long time. This is the last night of the World Series and an awards banquet is on. Going in for the awards is the only formal break in the long game: Under the rules, a player can be away from the table for thirty minutes to go to the bathroom or grab a bite to eat; after that he must put $100 into every pot until he gets back. So there are no two-hour lunch breaks.

It isn't long before Pug, Texas Dolly, and I are back at it. The game's getting fast. Besides anteing $50 each, all three of us are forcing the pot for $200, which amounts to a $350 ante before the cards are dealt.

I'm at my best during fast play. If one of these cats weakens to me, why, goddamn him, I'll take his money. If you show any weakness at this table, there'll be a seat open where *you* were sitting mighty quick. Show any weakness in your voice, in your actions, and you're gone. Here, I'm not only going to make them guess if I got a hand (and guessers are losers, neighbor); I'll make it look like a bluff if I do have a hand.

I look down in a minute and see that I've run that scrawny $1,775 up to $22,600. I'm now just a little shy of having a third of the chips on the table. Texas Dolly's got the most, Pug's second, and I've still got the least.

At this point, a friend of mine drops by. He looks a little anxious. He says solemnly, "Say, Slim, a man just laid me $8,000 to $5,000 that you don't win it."

"Well," I say to myself, "the odds are getting a little better anyway."

"This guy says you got it back up in pretty good shape," my pal explains. "He thinks you're probably the best player left in there, but you're still on the short end of the chips."

"Well, my God, boy—I'm really pulling for you to win it," I tell him with some flourish.

"You better be, damn it—you got half of it!" And he walks off.

So here's my predicament: This friend has bet an extra $2,500 for me on my winning, and I didn't even have a chance to say if I wanted that side bet. My motive is really growing, with that $2,500 to $100 bet I took earlier, plus what's on the table.

The play goes on. By now I've whittled down Texas Dolly to $20,100. And suddenly, Texas Dolly is sick—I mean *real* sick. He's running at both ends. We all agree to a thirty-minute break. It soon becomes obvious to the casino executives that Texas Dolly can't continue in the game because of illness. Under the World Series rules, he would forfeit his money, and he readily agrees to this. But he and I are past partners, and I don't feel like taking $20,000 off a guy with whom I've done that much business. Pug and I talk it over and agree to continue with the chips that are on the table, letting Texas Dolly keep his $20,100. With television and the formality that exists now, you would never see this in tournaments today, but this was still like a gathering of old friends.

With the playoff down to the two of us, the ante goes up to $100. Pug, by the way, is an ex–pool hustler like me, but we've got different poker styles. I clown a lot when I'm playing, and I'm always yakking with the kibitzers at the rail, which irks the hell out of Pug, since he knows it is part of my psychological strategy in poker games. If I can get a guy to listen to me, it will be to his misfortune.

"You better play 'em tight, you skinny son of a bitch, because I'm going to break you before the night's over," Pug warns.

I give him a big grin. "Take your best shot, partner. I been broke in bigger towns than Vegas, and lost to better men than you."

But Pug's making the best hands now. I don't make nothing. And if I try to steal a hand, he calls me.

"I like you, Pug," I tell him, "but I'll put a rattlesnake in your pocket and ask you for a match."

This brings a scowl and a grunt.

It's not going well for me. I guess I'm a little fatigued, having played for two days and two nights in another game before this one, with only about six hours sleep between. So I take my first break at the snack bar and order a glass of buttermilk. Then I go to the little boys' room and piss off about half of those seventy cups of coffee I've drunk during the game. I douse my hands and face in cold water, which perks me up a little.

I get after Pug. We've been anteing the $100 and *darkening the pot* for $200. If Pug puts in $200, I put in $400. The way we are playing, it's always up to him. He huddles with some of his cohorts, and I hear one of them tell him, "That Slim son of a bitch is straddling you every time you come in—you can't let him do that and win." Now, this is true. You can't stay straddled and win.

After this advice from his pals, it's soon evident that Pug means to take charge. After I put in $200, he comes out with $400 all of a sudden. So I top that with $800 in the dark—and that's unheard of.

I've got $1,100 in that pot and don't even have a hand.

Pug can see that to straddle me it will cost him $1,600, and he doesn't care to play that fast. But I'm a fast player: I'd play a banjo when a game's shorthanded. So I'm making my fast game work for me. If I have a hand, I raise; if I have a cold bluff, I raise. The way Pug plays tells me a lot. When he has to give first indication on his hand, I figure it this way: If I've raised it—and it comes a king, a queen, and a trey on the flop—and Pug decides to play, I know within reason that the king or queen hit him, since I raised the pot going in. If he passes, it doesn't make any difference if I have an eight and a four—that king is not important to me—I bet him $1,500. During the head-knocking between us, I'm all in—all my chips—on seven different hands. Pug never has all his chips in.

One time I feel sure that Pug is going to break me. I make an awful big bluff at him: He bets me $5,200 and I raise him $12,000, with no hand. I can't beat an egg, and I know he's going to call. I believe it's the first time that he senses I don't have a hand. It's the first time during all of this that he ever counts out his chips—the exact amount of chips to call the bet.

"My God Almighty," I'm thinking to myself. "I hope he don't call." But he *dogs it* and throws his hand away.

Another one of those cliff-hangers comes up, but he pitches in the best hand. Of course, that's the mark of a good player: anybody who can't quit the best hand can't play. But now I feel that he's going to call me the next big bet that I make.

I'm playing fast and taking Pug's money when I'm holding no

hand at all. Jimmy the Greek leans over and whispers to Pug. I've got mighty keen hearing. The Greek tells Pug I'm taking the money without a hand.

I make up my mind at this point: The first time that I make a hand—what I think probably is the winning hand—I'm going to sell it to him real high, playing it just like the bluffs I've been taking him with all along.

When the next hand comes, I get the king of hearts and the jack of clubs. *Pugs holds two sixes.* The pot's raised and reraised, with $1,400 above the ante in there. The flop comes an 8-8-K. I'm first action after the flop. If this boy's got a hand now, I'm going to break him. So instead of making him a sensible bet—like $1,500 or $2,000—I move in, betting him $51,000, although you ordinarily wouldn't sell the hand that I had anywhere nearly that high. You might sell it for $2,000 and then quit if you get played back at; but knowing he was fixing to call me the first time he got anything because he knows I've been running bluffs, I decide to use this to my advantage. Pug doesn't stall long: With $8,900 left, he covers that much of my bet, and he's all in for the first—and last—time.

The dealer flips over the last two cards. The first one off is an eight. Now Pug's dead in the pot. The last card is a blank that means nothing. I've made eights full of kings, which ends the game for Pug and his eights full of sixes. The entire game has lasted thirty-eight hours.

There's confusion everywhere now—cameras going off, microphones stuck in my face, people slapping me on the back, laughing, shouting.

Later, they tell me that I showed the first real jubilance I'd shown in the game: I always act happy as hell when I'm playing anyway. I get to a phone and call my family in Amarillo; I yell, "I won it!"

It's about three in the morning. I'm standing outside the Horseshoe; the air is hot and dry, and there aren't many people outside, except those still milling around the casino. I'm already a little disgusted: I've been looking two hours for another game.

My buddy Thackrey joins me. I push my hat back and sigh. "I'm looking for a game—any game at all, as long as it's for real money. Seems like a feller should be able to get a game like that—something interesting, you know—in a town like this. But I swear to goodness I just can't find a thing to occupy my time!"

"Goddamn it, Slim, you just won $60,000 in the World Series of Poker!"

"But that was *then*, and this is *now*. Feller like me, he's kind of like a doctor or a lawyer: you know, pretty near the only stock in trade that he's got is his time."

Well, that tournament was thirty-three years ago, and I still look forward to it every year. Of course, now that TV has taken hold of poker, it's turned into more of a circus and a lottery than an exclusive gathering, but it's still the biggest game in town, and I damn sure still want to win it!

POKER ETIQUETTE
Some Dos and Don'ts

Etiquette may be a highfalutin word for a poker player to use, but there are some dos and don'ts of conduct that are accepted more or less as standard behavior among poker players all over the world. Perhaps the toughest lesson in etiquette that I ever learned took place in Merry Old England, where they really do play like gentlemen (even though the basic idea still is to take your money). It has been said that I talk a lot when I play, and that's the truth for sure; but there is a good reason why I do this. If I'm not involved in the pot, I don't talk to the players who are; but if I am a participant, I talk to the other players because I'm hunting for a weakness in their conversation or some sort of a tell that will indicate what a player is holding. Or I may just be giving those people in the pot a snow job about a hand that I don't have. So the talking is part of my poker psychology, as I've explained earlier. There were, however, two instances in my life where talking really hurt me, and both happened in a high-stakes game in London.

It's a foggy day in old London town, where I'm playing in the Curzon Club. Now, British poker is quite a bit stricter than ours anyway, and there is one rule that prohibits talking while you're playing your hand. There are only three things you can say when it is your turn to act: "call," "pass," or "raise"—no more, no less. If you open your mouth at the wrong time in one of these English poker games, neighbor, somebody will put his foot in it.

In this particular game, I've got one of those British cats locked up cold turkey. He makes a good bet, but I want to stall and sell him my hand because I know I've really got him.

So the dealer says to me, "It is up to you, sir."

I answer, "Just hold on a minute there, partner. I think I got me a big pair down here in this hole." I act as though I were looking at my hand to make sure of what I've got, when suddenly they count me out of the pot.

"What the hell's going on here—I haven't passed!" I protest. And I sure as hell didn't intend to pass: I intended to vacate that boy's chair over there.

So a really smooth cat answers, "I'm sorry, sir, but that is cheating."

"Cheating? What the hell do you mean, cheating?" I demand.

This polished dude tells me that it is a "word-of-mouth" kind of cheating—that by talking about a big pair I may have in the hole, I'm "falsifying" my hand, and one does not falsify one's hands in London poker games.

"You cannot discuss your hand, sir," this British Emily Post says. "You may only act on your cards." He seems on the edge of being a little put out.

"Oh, my God!" I moan. But my groaning doesn't do any damned good, so I accept the ruling and give up my money— very reluctantly, I might add.

We rock along, and I become interested in another good hand. Before I even stop to think, when the betting comes to me I tell everybody, "Uh-huh! I think I got this cat. I think I'll introduce him to Mr. More," reaching for my chips to push in *more* chips for a big raise.

Someone shouts, "Foul! Forfeit! Forfeit the pot!"

And forfeit it I did.

That was the tail end of my talking, too. Anyone who knew me would not have recognized old Silent Slim during the remainder of *that* game.

Those errors are good examples of why it's so important to know the rules at the start of the game you're playing in, in order to follow the accepted etiquette. You must learn to adjust to the rules of games in various places with players whom you may not know: and you must have a definite understanding about such practices as burning top cards, cutting the deck, the raise limits, the best hands, settling up, and getting a new deck if you ask for it. For instance, there are certain sections of the country where burning that top card when dealing is not practiced. In the games I play in, it is traditional to discard that top card at the start of each deal, right after the cut.

Another etiquette "do" that I think is important is to always shuffle the cards facedown. Being a hawk-eyed bastard, I can see a card if it has just been flashed, and anytime I can see a card, it's beneficial to me—whether that card concerns my hand or not. It will have to concern someone's hand later, so I take advantage of any card that is exposed to me.

Regarding the question of cutting the cards, I believe that it should be a plain and simple one-handed cut by the player immediately to the dealer's right. A one-handed cut always is best, because that way, there cannot be any hocus-pocus. If I were in a game and a player were cutting those cards two or three times with both hands, I'd be pretty wary of that cat, because he's either locating some cards on you, or else he's got some *strippers* down in that deck, and he's trying to pull certain cards to the top or to take them out of play.

However, logical as the cutting procedure I've described is, game rules concerning the cutting of the cards will vary around the country. For instance, sometimes right in the middle of a pot, somebody will say, "I wanna cut the cards! Lemme cut the cards!" Well, that's all right, but in high-stakes poker games, we don't play by that kind of rule. Except at the start of the deal, the only time that you can cut the cards in these high games is when a card is accidentally exposed. And the person calling for the cut cannot cut them unless he is to the immediate right of the dealer. The cutter is *always* the player to the dealer's right. You have probably played in games where Old So-and-So sitting way over there wants to cut the deck. Don't hand the deck over there—that just isn't proper—hand it to the person behind you for the cut, the player to your right.

Poker players shouldn't get into that bad habit of wanting to "cut the cards, cut the cards, cut the cards." People say that a cut dog has no pups, and that's the damn truth. That kind of cutting the cards every time you turn around is for people either hunting luck with their ass, or trying to cut off something with their hands; and all it does is slow down the game and cause everyone to want to cut the cards. It's always the same price in a poker deal. I don't care if you flip a coin four times in a row and it turns up heads every time—it's still an even chance that it will come up tails the next time. But a lot of people still keep yelling, "Cut! cut! cut!" trying to outguess the cards, when all they're doing really is tattletaling their hand. If some player asks for a cut before drawing one card, every poker player there knows he is trying to cut them off to make a flush; it is very stupid to ask to cut the cards in that situation.

Another question of etiquette that comes up frequently at a poker game is seating position—a player's location in relation to the dealer. Any good player wants the best seating position he can get, of course, especially if he knows the playing habits of the others in the game. For example, nobody wants to be to the immediate right of a fast player, like me, mainly because of my habit of raising a lot of pots, with the idea of getting people off guard and trapping them when I do make a big hand. The only fair way to handle this problem in any game is to draw cards for seating position. And whoever is unfortunate enough to draw that hot spot must sit there.

Arguments over what is the best hand also come up more frequently in poker games than you'd think. These arguments break out particularly when you're playing wild-card games. Perhaps somebody will want to know whether five of a kind beats a straight flush; I've played in games in which it does, while at other games, the straight flush was the top hand. So it is certainly important to have a complete understanding about these hands at the very beginning, *before* the situations come up.

A player always should be careful not to expose his cards, whether or not he is involved in a pot. If you quit a hand, throw your cards facedown in the discards, because if just one of them is shown, it could benefit another player still in that pot. Suppose a player has two queens in his hand and you accidentally flash a queen as you throw in. Knowing that one of his queens is gone, it is likely that he will fold now. Or say somebody has some kind of a flush draw, and you have two cards of his flush suit in your discards. If he sees them, he knows that instead of figuring his hand with nine winners in the deck, he now has only seven he can count on—and if it is seven instead of nine, why hell, that's nearly 20 percent the worst of it.

So don't let anybody see the cards—when you're shuffling, dealing, playing, or discarding. If you don't get a good facedown shuffle when you're mixing them up, cut those cards four or five times yourself. Just whack them off, and then hand them to the man behind you to cut one more time.

Another rule to observe is *never* rib a loser when you're playing poker: That is something that is definitely frowned on. You can laugh and joke and tease with everybody, but if Old So-and-So over there is losing his money, it's good fetching to let up on him. He's feeling bad enough anyway. Go ahead and beat the hell out of him, but don't rib him after you do it.

And never criticize another man's way of playing his hand. For instance, I don't like to be in a game with a tight player—an ultraconservative type who's waiting for the best hand before he gets into a pot—but I'll never openly criticize such a player. I believe that a man who buys his chips is entitled to play them any damn way he wants to. (Besides that, I'll take a tight player's money the first chance I get.)

Then, of course, there is your own conduct to be considered if you are a loser in a game. You've seen people who get mad as hell, tear up or throw the cards (or throw a little dog like the Lawyer did that time I beat him). Those kinds of tantrums are definitely a no-no. I've never torn up a deck of cards in my life, and I don't believe in *squeaking* if you lose.

In my many years of poker playing, I have never asked for a deck to be changed if it was in good condition. Of course, I've been in some games where the cards damn sure needed changing, when some cat over there might be bending the cards a little, or putting a little weight on them, or scratching the pasteboards up a little. I don't say too much about that kind of conduct—I live my own life in a poker game—but that card doctoring will surely help me as much as it will help the *thief* doing it.

But even if it's just that you're having a run of bad luck and for that reason you want a new deck of cards, you are entitled to one if you ask for it. Everybody sitting there is entitled to change the deck anytime he wants to. Now, I am not saying that it helps to switch to a new deck when you're not having any luck with the present deck; I just don't pay any attention to bad runs, because you make your own bad runs in poker.

As for the settling up in a poker game, that's something that always should be mountain-air clear before a game starts. I have to know how we are going to settle up before I get into any game; the only time I'm not interested in the settling-up procedure is when we're playing strictly for cash. (Of course, due to the numerous hijacks across America—and I'm speaking of poker games, not jetliners—we frequently don't play for cash in the big games in Texas because you get mighty tired of looking down those sawed-off shotgun barrels.)

Settling up is done differently in various places: It might be before the game, or after the game, or before next week's game. But be certain that it is definitely established *before* you take a hand. This avoids arguments and hurt feelings that may come up when one man is a big loser and another guy is sitting there wondering how he is going to collect the money he has won. I want to be sure that the money I'm playing for is there, if I win it. If a man says he'll give me his check, I would rather *not* have his check; it's better just to wait until the next day for the bank to open and do our playing then.

I've been in predicaments where the "etiquette," if you will call it that, was enforced; and though it may not have been to my liking, I still managed to find some advantage in it. I guess I'm kinda like that optimist who gets a big box of horseshit from some joker for his birthday, and when this optimist opens it up, he's happy as hell and starts digging in all that horse dung—looking for the horse.

One incident occurred in London, when my old friend Johnny Moss and I got wind of some high-stakes games. Somehow, though, the news of our arrival had preceded us; we had been checked into the London Hilton for only about four or five hours when we had some visitors we weren't expecting.

There is a knock at the door of our room, so I open it and see two big fellows standing there, neatly dressed but with pretty tight smiles on their faces. I know right away what they are—muscle. "You must be Amarillo Slim," one of the boys says, looking me up and down.

"Yep," I answer.

"Mind if we come in a minute, Slim?" he asks, and they come right on in without waiting for an answer. "This must be Mr. Johnny Moss," the same guy says, stopping in front of Johnny. His sidekick hasn't said anything yet.

"Yep," says Mr. Moss.

"We are glad to see you gentlemen here, and we want to welcome you," the muscle says. "Do you plan to be gambling while in our city?"

"Yeah, that's right, I am for goddamned sure," I say.

Then these two English muscle boys tell us all about ourselves—they have a lot of background, and they know that Johnny and I are ranked among the top poker players in America. At the same time, they convey their authority to us, politely pointing out that in order for us to play in London, it will be necessary that we cut in the people they represent for 25 percent.

Johnny, who was a small bundle of dynamite with a short-fused temper, goes through the ceiling. He cusses and tells them to go to hell while they stand there with those tight, head-breaking smiles on their faces. I interrupt Johnny's tirade. "Hey, Johnny, slow down a minute—let's see what the hell this is all about." In my own mind, I know these damn cats mean business, and though they don't carry guns in England (it is a felony), they do their work with some other tools when they get mad. Just for openers, they're liable to pin your hands to a table with hatchets.

So the muscle does some more talking, while Johnny still sputters in the background, and then they happen to mention what for me are the magic words: They guarantee that I'll get any money that I win. Now, that guaranteed settling up means something to a country boy like me in a foreign land. If I'm going to play some guy who's a $10,000 man, I know he's good for it up to that ten grand, but I can't be sure of any amount over that. And I like to pull out the stops when I'm playing. If a guy loses $10,000 to me and wants to keep going in the game, that would be just fine now, because if he welshes and doesn't pay me what he owes me, I know *these* people will make it good. And he has to pay them, believe me, he has to pay them!

Looking at the overall picture, 75 percent of the pie looks better to me than no pie at all. You might say it's a form of insurance, my taking this deal (which I don't have any choice about anyway). I know that I won't get hurt if I go along; I know nothing will happen to me as long as they have 25 percent of my take. And I know from experience that when muscle moves in, you've either got their blessing or you don't play in their territory. And if I don't take this offer and go ahead and play, I'll have some trouble—and I just wouldn't care for one of those concrete life jackets or a hatchet wrapped around my bony old head.

I suppose muscle is a necessary evil in this business. Now, don't get me wrong, neighbor. These types of people are not my associates and I don't approve of what they do. Yet if it is convenient for me to use them to my benefit, then I love to use them.

The arrangement suited me just fine in the long run. Johnny went home, and these people put me in some games I would not have known about otherwise. There wasn't anything crooked about these games, mind you—they were on the up and up—but these people received 25 percent of my playing.

As far as I'm concerned, they can do their thing and I'll do mine, and it will be a peaceful coexistence. The London visit proved to be a very satisfactory one for me—and for them. I carried some of those monied bookmakers whom I played a lot farther than I would have ordinarily—I let them drown their own filly—because I knew I'd get my money.

So you see, sometimes the rules of poker etiquette require a little compromising of your usual procedures. That way, you leave good feelings behind you, you can come back and play again, and—as in my case—you stay alive.

ONLINE POKER

The minute Chris Moneymaker, a twenty-seven-year-old working stiff from Tennessee who had never played in a live poker tournament in his life, turned a $40 satellite entry from Pokerstars.com into $2.5 million in cash for winning the World Series of Poker in 2003, everyone took notice that online poker was for real. Heck, if you had told me five years ago that people would play poker for money in a place where you couldn't look a man in the eye, I would have told you that what you smelled cooking wasn't on the fire.

As I write this in 2005, PokerStars.com has 1.3 million registered players and they're only number two in the market behind PartyPoker.com. My uneducated country ass even got a computer, but after trying to play online a couple times, I nearly threw it clear through a plate-glass window. Even though it's not for me, if you're a poker player today, you at least need to be aware that you can always find a game online.

I told you about all the money I lost while I was learning poker, and it's almost inevitable that your poker education is going to be costly. Even if you read all the books, you'll need to play thousands of hands before you can get a feel for the game. With online poker, you can now get the education for free! All the online poker rooms have games with play money. And once you get comfortable with that, you can start playing for nickels and dimes and gradually work your way up to a level where you can win some real money.

The best thing about online poker—aside from being able to play in your Jockey shorts—is that you play about twice as many hands an hour as you do in a casino (and probably four times as many than when you're playing with your friends). The speed of the game gives you the chance to play more hands in a shorter period of time and hone your skills. Many players will play more than one game at once, and I heard that Phil Ivey, one of the top players in the world right now, plays seven games at a time!

The biggest difference between live games and online games, of course, is that you can't look a player in the eye to get a read. The other thing you've got to remember is that you have to be in a poker frame of mind when you sit down to play and find a way to block out all the distractions. Whether you realize it or not, you take steps to prepare yourself to play poker when you walk into a cardroom. Even if you're only traveling across a casino from your hotel room to the poker room, you're involved in a change of space, and this physical transition naturally brings about a mental transition as well. Online, it's different. You can go from plunging the toilet to posting a blind in the time it takes to click "bad beat." If you make the jump into online play without proper mental preparation, you run the risk of playing poorly to start and digging yourself a hole right away.

I also think there's some psychology at play that tends to turn people into worse players online—which means that if you're paying attention, neighbor, there's an opportunity for you to win. If you lose a big pot in a live game, you see those chips go away and you see your stack get smaller. Online, the only thing that changes is a number on a screen. It's all too easy to treat that number as insignificant, all too easy not to feel the loss deep down in your gut, where it counts. When that happens—when you don't feel the emotional impact of losing—you run the risk of not caring whether you win or lose. Don't be the one to fall into that trap. Whether it's chips or graphics, money is money, and you need to play to win at all times—in any poker game.

Another thing to keep in mind is that your flaws could actually hurt you less online, because the online environment doesn't give them a chance to do damage. So if you have great discipline and a solid knowledge of odds but are terrible at picking up tells, or, worse, you have an awful poker face, playing online will highlight your strengths and hide your weaknesses.

I also don't think you can forget that peer pressure is something that actually makes bad players play better when they're in a cardroom. The fear of being laughed at for starting with bad cards or drawing to a long shot causes them to play a little bit better. You'll often hear players joke about how they're embarrassed to be playing a certain hand or how they "hope they don't have to turn this one up." In a game with players who play to impress as much as they do to win, it's the fear of being thought of as a sucker that actually makes people play better. Online, where everyone is anonymous, that element goes straight out the window.

The good news is that it can have a negative effect on your opponents' play. The bad news is that it can have a noticeable negative effect on *your* play. But if you're reading this book, you've at least proven that you *want* to be a winner, and I trust you'll make the right adjustments.

Five years ago, Internet poker didn't exist. Now it's a wild frontier of nonstop action as players—and companies—from every corner of the globe fight for their share of the big bucks floating around in cyberspace. If you play online, there's a lot of dead money out there for you to collect. If you don't, and you're an opportunistic poker player, how much longer can you put it off? But shoot, don't ask me that question. Ask Chris Moneymaker and Greg Raymer.

TOURNAMENTS

$\mathcal{B}$ack when I was playing pool, we used to joke that the people who won tournaments were the ones who wanted their picture in the paper. As a pool hustler, that was the *last* thing on earth I wanted. Even in poker, it never did you any good to advertise the fact that you were winning. In fact, I would always go out of my way to talk about what a sucker I was and dress the part of the hayseed country cowboy.

Nowadays, it's a new world where poker players have become like rock stars and professional athletes. A friend of mine showed me an article from ESPN.com in which Phil Hellmuth Jr. was asked if there's more money to be played *playing* poker or *endorsing* poker. Naturally, Phil said the latter because, if truth be told, he's as soft as butter at the poker table. Of course, I'm only half kidding, and the fact that Phil has won nine events at the World Series, including the World Championship in 1989, has made him rich and famous and given him the opportunity to make all that money in endorsements. There are a hundred players better than

Phil making money in cash games across the country who will never get the recognition and, even worse, have to go to battle every day to win their daily bread while Phil cashes checks based on his celebrity.

If your goal is to earn recognition, then you've got to play in tournaments. If you want to be a superstar with a team of agents, your own clothing line, and your picture in the newspaper, play as many as you can.

The second reason to play a tournament is obvious: You can parlay a small investment into a big score. And now, with all the satellites and supersatellites, you can parlay a *real small* investment into a huge score. It certainly makes sense for any poker player to try to pull a Moneymaker and enter some $40 satellites with a chance to get a seat in the World Series of Poker.

I also think that before entering any tournament, you should play at least one satellite. If you don't already know, a satellite is a small tournament whereby the winner gets a seat into a bigger tournament. At the World Series of Poker, for example, ten players will pay $1,000 (plus about $60 in juice to the house) and play a one-table tournament. The last one standing gets a seat in the main event.

The reason to play a satellite goes beyond leveraging $1,000 into a multimillion-dollar payday. What it does is give you experience playing at a final table—the most important table at any tournament. You'll quickly learn that there are certain players who are playing to survive and others who are playing to win. The ones who are trying to survive I run over like a pebble on a Texas highway. While they're trying to *preserve* their chips, I'm accumulating them.

As for specific tournament strategy, I'm going to have to leave that to my peers. That Ivy League math whiz David Sklanksy has written a solid book called *Tournament Poker for Advanced Players* that can't be ignored. T. J. Cloutier, who I have faced many times both in Texas and at tournaments in the World Series of Poker, has also written several great books. Any champion who can also write is not to be ignored.

What I can tell you is that the biggest difference between live play and tournaments is that you can't buy more chips once you bust out of a tournament (certain tournaments do have rebuys, but they all reach a point where once you bust out, you're gone). That's why you have to think a lot about your stack size. Poker is all about exploring small edges, so if I'm playing a cash game where I have the best of it, I'm going to put as much money as I can in the pot. If I lose, I'll buy more chips and keep looking for opportunities to get my money in the pot when I have the best of it.

In tournaments, on the other hand, if I'm a small favorite over a player and he checks to me and all I have left is enough for one bet, I'm not going to put that money in the pot. I'd rather give up a small edge so as not to put myself in a position to be *eliminated*. Remember, once you get to the final table, your goal is to *win*, but before you get to the final table, your goal is to *survive*.

The World Series of Poker is now a seven-day tournament, and let me let you in on a little secret: You can't win it on the first day! Yes, you want to accumulate chips and give yourself a cushion, but you don't want to do so at the risk of being eliminated. So based on that, I'm not going to tell you just to play your normal game—you have to pay attention to your stack size.

What you've also picked up on, I'm sure, is that the other players are thinking about their stack size. Especially now that you have all these amateurs playing in tournaments, most of them just want to survive and tell their friends that they lasted a long time. Well, if you can pick out those players, those are the ones you want to *attack*. Because they're playing so scared and thinking only about survival, you'll be able to bluff them a lot.

If a tournament is paying thirty places, finishing in thirty-first place is known as finishing on the *bubble*. Well, when you get down to about forty players, you've got five or six (including me) who are thinking about winning the damn thing, and the rest are just trying to finish in the money. This is the time that players get overly conservative, so you can really bluff them.

If you're playing in a World Poker Tour event, in which only the final six make the final table that is shown on TV, players start getting very tight and nervous as soon as you get down to a dozen or so. Again, *attack, attack, attack* and take advantage of their conservative play.

In the old days, just about all the tournaments were winner-take-all, but now the payout structure is such that a lot more players walk away with something. But even so, usually 30 to 40 percent goes to the winner and 70 to 80 percent goes to the top four or five. That's why you have to play to win! Those who are just trying to move up from ninth to eighth usually end up in ninth or eighth, while those playing to win pick up their chips.

Tournaments are all the rage now, and there's so much money out there that you've got to take your shots. Always try to get in cheap with a satellite, and then once you're there, play to survive until the final table and play to win once you're there.

THE LIFE *of a* POKER-PLAYING MAN

*S*ure, I call myself a gambler, and I'm damn proud to have made my living by my wits for seventy-six years, but if truth be told, I'm really more of a businessman who looks for opportunities to invest my money when the odds are in my favor. That's why you'll never see me put one nickel in a slot machine, on the craps table, or on a lottery ticket.

To be a great poker player, you must be disciplined and have self-control. That's why it still amazes me that some of the world's greatest poker players have so little discipline when they're away from the felt. Money that leaves your bankroll for reckless purposes is called a *leak*. For poker players, sports betting, craps, blackjack, and drugs are at the top of this list. It's estimated that Stuey Ungar, perhaps the greatest poker player—and without a doubt the greatest gin player—who ever lived, made more than $30 million playing cards in his career, yet he died with only $800 and countless debts to his name. Gambling on the golf course, in the pit, on sports, and on horses poked holes in Stuey's pocket. So did drugs, which ultimately took his life. And it's a damn shame.

Ironically, it was Stuey who said, "But gambling for a living isn't something you fill out a job application for. It's a rough life. It's an unstable life. It has its hazards. Plenty. So many hazards, in fact, that gambling is something very few people can do successfully. And if you have a leak in your game, whatever it is, this town [Las Vegas] is going to eat you alive."

That's the truth, neighbor. Because for all the good advice I've given you in this book, it can really mess with your mind when you sit there patiently, play great poker, and then lose a big chunk of your bankroll when someone hits a 40-to-1 shot against you. It happens every day, and it's a rare person who can accept it, move on, and *still* play great poker. That's why it's my advice to you that you play poker to win and create an income for yourself, but don't put yourself in a position where it's the only way you pay your bills. There's just too much stress and too good of a chance that the pressure will lead you to some of those awful leaks.

An item from the February 17, 1970, Sydney (Australia) *Sun*, written by Bill Casey, called ". . . and Nobody Asked for swy!" reported:

> The late, great Runyon, once had a character, the gambler Sky Masterson, speak on the matter to Nathan Detroit. "The Sky" said that his father, being a little short of anything else, had bankrolled him with the following advice. "One day a man will come along with a deck of cards, of which the seal is unbroken, and will want to bet you that the Jack of Spades will jump out of that pack and squirt ci-

der in your ear. Do not bet him son, for you will surely finish up with an ear full of cider." Events around the sporting circles over the past week in Sydney have proved just how right Mr. Masterson was.

Half the sports around town are currently washing cider out of their ears, and boy, has it been an expensive drop.

A little over a week ago two amiable young fellows were introduced to the big boys of Sydney's sporting fraternity.

They were obviously American, as they wore ten gallon hats and spoke with a nice easy Texas drawl. They were immediately popular with members, particularly when they displayed a partiality for a small wager now and again.

"Do you play snooker?" they were asked.

"Certainly, suh, I'd be delighted," said one of the Texans.

If you happen to know anything about snooker, you probably think it is nigh on impossible for anyone to spot someone else 80 start if that someone else knows which end of the cue is for chalking.

But there is a well-known chap around town who cannot only give practically anybody 80 start, but play them left-handed, too. Supporters of this remarkable cueist now wish they had never met those Americans.

Some hours after the challenge at one of our leading clubs, their man had still not won a game, and pockets were emptied to the extent of hundreds of dollars.

Last night someone suggested a game of gin rummy, and would you believe it, one of the Texans did play a little. There are some exceptional exponents of gin rummy in Sydney, and a game was soon set up.

Thinking that it wouldn't hurt to take a little of the wind from the U.S. sails, the stakes suggested were $1,000 a game.

To the surprise of all, this was accepted with remarkable alacrity. And around six hours later, one of those ten gallon hats was filled with practically every loose dollar within reach.

I am now told that our American friends would have trouble getting a game of marbles, even if it is a big-ring.

But they are quite willing to buy the cider. . . .

The jaunt to Sydney, Australia, started like most of the fortune-prospecting journeys I make—with a rumor that some high poker was being played there. I'll go anywhere in the world for high action, especially if it is up in the six-figure bracket. Word of these games gets around; somebody will call me at home, or wherever I may be, or contact a casino in Nevada that knows where to get in touch with me.

In this case, a man phoned me and said, "Slim, they're playing some poker in Sydney, Australia, and it's supposed to be a hell of a good game. Whatta you doing?" I was in Nevada at the time, and I wasn't very busy. It sounded like a good thing to me, so I told this boy, "Nothing, neighbor. I'd like to go down that way anyhow, because I want to buy some horses."

There was a short pause. "I don't have any money, Slim."

"You don't need any, partner," I replied. I stopped off in Amarillo just long enough to get my passport, which looks like a chicken scratched on it because of all the places I've been, and then this feller and I took a jet to Sydney. Since he was broke, I furnished the money. But we didn't know we were heading for a disappointment.

When we arrived, what we smelled cooking was not on the fire. Once again, though, this big western hat and these cowboy boots of mine saved the day. I went to the racetrack, and I wasn't there very long before I met the kind of people I'm always looking for. Through them I found out about an exclusive club in Sydney, and I got an invitation to pay it a visit.

When I entered the club, I noticed a six-by-twelve snooker table and some tables covered with green felt, which looked downright promising. It wasn't very long before I learned they had a world-champion snooker player as a club member. They asked me if I ever played snooker; well, they didn't know it, but that was kind of like asking Howard Cosell if he ever broadcast any sporting events.

I not only cut my teeth on a pool cue in Amarillo, where I eventually became the snooker champion, but I shot snooker and hustled pool games up and down the West Coast while a young man serving in the U.S. Navy; and later, I traveled all over Europe as a civilian member of Uncle Sam's Special Services, giving pool exhibitions and chalking up with the champions of the world. This is my background, and I told these Sydney gents, "Yes, suh, I'd be delighted to try my hand at some snooker."

Well, I really dusted this champion of theirs playing snooker. Things got so exciting between him and me that the Harlem Globetrotters, who were playing an exhibition game in Sydney, quit at the half and came upstairs to watch our snooker game because there was no one left watching them.

After I got this snooker behind me, my partner and I were asked to join the card playing. That, of course, was what I had been waiting for, and we played gin rummy and poker, too. I went "down under" to stay ten days and ended up staying six weeks! There is a rumor that I came away with a lot of money on that trip; but what's more, I am welcome back—they even made me an honorary member of that club. The boy who went with me is not welcome back. It turns out he was a thief and a *cheat*, something I sure as hell didn't know when I was paying his way.

Sometimes people wonder about my background, if I come from a long line of professional gamblers. Nothing could be further from the truth. My folks were average, churchgoing, hardworking people. Daddy ran some cafés and a used-car business in Amarillo for many years.

I was born in Johnson, Arkansas, but my folks saw the error of their ways and came to Texas when I was less than a year old. I grew up in Texas and consider myself a dyed-in-the-wool Texan. My folks divorced when I was about eleven, and I spent part of the time with one, and then the other.

There was no gambling background at all in the family. When I was in high school in Amarillo, I used to cut sixth-period study hall with three other boys (one who became a candidate for mayor of our town in later years), and I'd go to the pool halls and bust everybody playing pool.

That's the way it all got started. First pool, and then I got interested in cards. I guess I was about sixteen years old at the time, and I was always looking for a new chance or a new way to make money. At that time, the money was important, but nowadays, money is just a toy to me—it's the thrill and the challenge of beating the best that I'm after. I don't have any set amount of money that I want to make.

As a young man, I had a keen eye and a sharp wit, and I got into games in places where other people couldn't. I started out as a pool hustler, and I became the best in my town and later played all over the country, too. I generally was "undercover" when hustling pool—I wore the cowboy hat and boots and played the role of the country kid who thinks he can shoot pool. By the time I was seventeen years old, I'd played practically all the good players in the United States. Most of them beat me then, primarily because of my youth. But from seventeen on, I became quite proficient in pool.

I joined the Navy when I was seventeen. The Navy recruiting team had come around while I was in high school and explained that anyone who had a C average could join up and get a high school diploma. It was a good deal in the Navy: I was a captain's yeoman and chauffeur, and that wasn't a hell of a lot of work, so with all that free time, I hustled pool up and down the West Coast, using a Navy vehicle. (It definitely was against the rules and regulations, yet because of this Navy vehicle, I had gas available during the war, and I had all the chow I wanted and could stay in the fine hotels for free.) It was really something: I won five Cadillac automobiles in San Francisco in one week just playing pool—I won the Caddys after winning all the surplus money that was sewed up there.

After my tour in the Navy, I thought I had all the money there was in the world—I just couldn't imagine anybody else having any left over. I had over $100,000 when I came out of the Navy. Well, it lasted me just over a year. I was still just a kid, not quite twenty.

After I went broke, this chance came along to enter the U.S. Special Services. In this job, I gave pocket billiards exhibitions throughout the European theater, and again I had a lot of spare time over there, too. I was supposed to have been a goodwill ambassador, and I guess I probably did create a little goodwill. But by the same token, I busted all those GIs playing poker and shooting craps and betting on the football games—making wagers on anything that was competitive.

I stayed in Special Services almost a year. While I was on these tours, I played all the European champions: Erich Hagenlacher, the European balk line billiards champion, in Germany; in France, the international European three-pocket billiards champion, Roger Conti; and Joe Davis of England, the world champion snooker player. (I never beat him.)

I beat Hagenlacher at snooker because he was primarily a billiards player. I had to play billiards with Conti. I didn't know billiards and he beat me, and I told him I was tired of having him beat me. He answered, "Well, you just can't play." I told him, "I *can* play, if we lay some money on the line and if we can find a table that's got pockets on it." Before I left France, I won several thousand francs off that man because we finally went to a town where I found me a snooker table. Well, I knocked all the tail feathers out of him playing snooker, and from then on, when he and I played an exhibition game, it got a little closer. He used to beat me unmercifully, but after I broke his ass at snooker, he let up on me a little in the exhibition games.

I kept playing pool until I was about thirty years old. Yes, I've also played Minnesota Fats, first in Perth Amboy, New Jersey, where Fats beat me out of $12,000. Then, in 1950, he came to Amarillo and played me, and I broke him and three of his backers. I played Fats again in Atlanta, Georgia, and he broke me. I have played him three times in all, and he beat me two of them. The first time Fats played me, he didn't know who I was; he beat me out of that $12,000, but he could have won five times that amount. After I left, he found out who I was, and then he came to Amarillo and played me a proposition game, and I beat him—took his money and that of the three backers he brought with him.

Pool was good for me; it was very lucrative right after the war, but then it died out. The big money went to cards, so I adapted myself. My occupation is still listed on my tax returns as professional pool player, and I played in three world tournaments every year through the mid-1970s.

I thrive on the action and excitement of high-stakes poker. My way of life is satisfying to me—and a man has to like his line of work. Folks have asked me why I never did "get into something else." Hell, that's a silly question as far as I'm concerned. What should I get into—something I don't know a damned thing about—maybe building computers or inventing medical wonder drugs or being a college professor? Would the world be better off if I made myself unhappy by opening up a shoe store or an automobile garage?

I'm not what some of the young people would call "goal oriented." I'm not looking for as much money as H. L. Hunt or Howard Hughes. I've got no specific amount I'm aiming for; money, as I've said, is just a way of keeping score. I'm enjoying the trip as I go along, having a good time and trying to make my family and the people I like happy, too. Most of the things in the world that I want are things that I have—how many people can say that? I enjoy gambling, and I don't hurt a soul doing it (I won't play some old boy who makes $2,000 a month at a service station), and there is no one who can tell me that that's the wrong way to go. If the world were to end tomorrow—or if *I* ended tomorrow—I would not regret a bit of it. Not one damn thing!

Seems like card players get all the notoriety, but how many people do you know who go to the golf course and have some kind of wager riding on it every time they tee off? It might be only a dime a hole, and yet they're as guilty of gambling as I am in any high-stakes poker game. I might add I bet like hell on the golf course myself, but am I any more guilty because I bet $10,000 than some guy who bets $3? Still, they're supposed to be goody-goodies, and I'm the villain. I sure as hell don't feel that way about the life I lead.

No way around it, the life of a professional poker player *is* an interesting life. Yes, there are times when you're going to get busted flat on your ass. Nobody is always a winner, and anybody who says he is, is either a liar or doesn't play poker.

I was down South one time in a game with a bunch of the top players. One guy had lost a lot of money and he was squeaking, really squeaking. There were about six of us who went to a place to eat, while this boy was squeaking about his losses. There was no denying that he had lost a hell of a lot of money. Now, most professional gamblers don't squeak when they lose, but he kept on and on. Finally, I said to him "Where'd you get that suit?"

"It's a tailor-made suit," he said.

"What'd it cost you?" I asked. Now keep in mind this was forty years ago, when a hundred dollars actually meant something.

"Three hundred and fifty-nine dollars," he said.

"What's that you're wearing on your feet, partner?" I asked.

"Those are alligator loafers."

"How much they cost ya?"

"A hundred and fifty dollars."

I said, "You got on a pair of cashmere socks. What'd they set you back?"

"Six dollars a pair."

I asked him what he was paying for the suite he was occupying in the hotel.

"Forty dollars a night," he said.

"You flew down here in a jetliner, didn't you?"

He admitted that was so.

"What'd we just order now?" I asked. We were sitting at a table in a restaurant.

"Prime rib." He was beginning to look rather sheepish. Prime rib was $7.50.

I said, "All right, now lookee here, neighbor. You're wearing a $360 tailor-made suit, you've got on a pair of $150 shoes, you paid $6 for those socks, you're staying in a $40-a-night suite, you flew here on a jet, you're eating a $7.50 piece of meat, and you're hollering? How many people do you know who do all that?"

I know I live high on the hog, but it's something you have to do when you're hunting high-stakes poker. I wear both shop-made and tailor-made western suits that cost up to $1,000 a suit; I have a dozen or so pairs of boots, including calf, kangaroo, ostrich, anteater, lizard, alligator, and nylon, that run from $225 to $1,000 a pair and up; and probably a dozen expensive ten-gallon hats. I've owned a stable of racehorses, but they were a liability, not an asset. I've had some ventures in the stock market that were all bad. But I'm not looking for a solid investment. My investments will be to bet on the next World Series or Super Bowl.

I have done most of my globe-trotting and poker playing during the winter months, while I spent the summers with my family. I lead an ordinary family man's life; I've even coached Little League baseball.

One time I was playing in Nevada and a man who I know is with the Organization (read between the lines here, partner) came over and asked for a piece of my play. I know these people; I won't deny it. But the extent of my association with them is "Hi" and "How are you?" They respect me because they know my word is good, that I'll do what I say I'll do. I laugh and I joke with these people, and they accept it that way. So, instead of just telling this Organization feller he couldn't have a piece of my play, I told him I already had five partners. He slapped me on the back and walked off, and one of the guys sitting at the table asked, "Whatta you mean, Slim, you got five partners?"

"I damn sure do," I said, grinning. "I got a wife, three kids, and a Weimaraner dog." My idea is that you catch more flies with honey than you do with vinegar. That way, you don't make enemies—and you can't afford to have those Organization people for enemies.

I'm always being asked what it takes to be a professional poker player. Well, you must have a strong constitution and no nerves whatsoever. And you have to be an honest man. All the stock in trade that a gambler has is his word. Most likely, he'll have his money somewhere in a safe-deposit box, but if he needs it to meet his bets, he'll go get it or send for it. And he'll pay his gambling debts before he pays his grocery bill. And if you don't, well, it doesn't take six months in this business to find out who will and who won't. We're always running into one another—us high-stakes players—wherever we go. And word gets around fast— "Old So-and-So got $2,000 from Old So-and-So, and the next time he saw him, he didn't pay him." That's the kiss-off, that feller is through in the big games because his word is no damn good.

It's a small, elite group of men who play big poker for a living. But you won't find a more honest group anywhere in the world. They are tough, hard-bitten guys who have been around; they know their way anywhere on this globe. And yet, in our circle, we can lay down beside one another and sleep and leave all our money in our pants pocket and not worry about it. You can't do that with the square johns.

In a room full of professional gamblers, we can walk off and leave all our chips on the table, even if we have to go back to the motel and change clothes, or leave the game to sleep for five or six hours. We don't worry a bit about somebody taking our chips. Now, go play in some of these private games with some of these Goody Two-shoes, and see how you come out if you leave your pile unattended for a minute. I've got two or three cigar boxes full of bad checks I've been given by businessmen, but I haven't got one from a professional gambler.

In our circle, when we get broke, we can borrow money in two different ways. We don't sign any notes—we don't sign anything at all. You either borrow *principle money*, or you borrow a bankroll with the understanding you'll pay it back when you can.

With principle money, you tell the sender *when* you are going to pay it back, and, neighbor, you pay it back exactly when you tell him. When you borrow the money without setting a repayment deadline, you may run into the lender the next day or the next week in a game. But he will not ask for or expect the money until you say when you'll have it—he knows you're short, or you'd pay it back.

But principle money is just what it says, because if you are short of cash and need your money—the money you need to operate on—and you have been told a time when you'll get the money back, that's when you're supposed to get it, no later. You pay the lender principle money the following morning or whenever you can get to your *stash* and get your money.

And with us, there's no such thing as interest. Of course, in certain towns there are loan sharks, but I've never gotten any money from them, and I've been broke more times than I've got hairs on my head. You just don't deal with those people. If I go broke, I'll get busy and go play in some games that ordinarily I would not get into because they are smaller stakes.

In this world today, nobody does any business any more without signing contracts, except professional gamblers. In the frontier days, a man's word was good enough for deals involving thousands of dollars, and it's still that way in our circle. In the old days, we'd often go partners on a trip. Say, for instance, that Texas Dolly heard that I was going to go on a playing trip. He might have been in Fort Worth and I'd be in Alaska, but he'd get on the phone and say, "Slim, I've got twenty-five percent of you while you're gone." That's the way it'd be, neighbor. And when I got back, if I won $14,000, he knew I wasn't going to tell him it was $8,000 and give him $2,000; and if I told him I lost, he knew that I did—there'd be no question. He'd simply assume 25 percent of that loss. If you ever get where you cannot operate that way in the gambling business, then you have no chance.

There is some gambling I will not do. I don't even know those crap tables are out there. I also will not play blackjack, because I know who has the best of it there—I know the percentages in gambling. And I know that if I play baccarat, I've got the worst of it. Now, I'm not knocking these games, because I'm around them all the time, but you have to be getting the worst of it when you play them, and I have to have the best of it.

I'm a winner—I play poker to win. My gambling philosophy is that the losers walk, the winners talk. There are winners and losers, and all my life I have been a winner.

In my dealings, I have found that the monied people in America are the biggest phonies. With them it's all a big "I" and a little "you." These big shots want to do this and do that, but I do very little business with them, either because I know something about them, or their word is no good. It is surprising how many people are being taken regularly in some of these private games. I play in them once in a while—people will call and want me to come to their hometown and sit in a game—and it doesn't take me long to see that these people are being robbed.

But I wouldn't tattletale on this robber. That's his thing, and I don't bother anyone. Yet I won't stand to be robbed myself, so I have a way of letting this thief know that I am wise to what he is and to what he's doing. This is more or less a courtesy among gamblers; if I am involved in a pot, he won't take the best of it with *me*, because if he does, he has to kick my money back. I am damned sure not going to lose my money to a man knowing that he is cheating me.

A man is a fool to do something like that. For one thing, there are only so many ways that a fellow can cheat at any game, and by this time, I think I know about most of them because most of them have been tried on me. But I have a standing offer to card cheats: Buy yourself a round-trip ticket from wherever you are to Amarillo. Then bring your money and come play me a game. And use any fool gimmick, any device, any trick you like. If you can get away with it, then you can keep what you win off me; but if I catch you, your bankroll stays in Amarillo and you use the other half of that round-trip ticket. However, I don't know any thief who really can play. If you take away his cheating, he cannot really do anything; so when I encounter one, I generally cause him some bad luck.

Another occupational hazard in our business is hijacks: We get held up every once in a while. But that's just one of the hazards of this business, because if we get hijacked, we don't say anything about it to the law. We're not looking to run and tell it.

Hijackers will hit the game or hit you after you leave. You are always pointed out, and they will be waiting for you at your room, or they will come and take off the whole game. I take some precautions, but I prefer not to say here what they are. I've been lucky—I've only been robbed for big money five or six times in my life. I missed one of the biggest ones; I was supposed to be at that game, but I wasn't there. That is why we don't play with cash in the high-stakes games anymore.

I look forward to the World Series of Poker every year. As long as they're holding it, you can bet your damn boots I'll be there. I hope a lot more card players around the country come out, too. All the local champions usually show up. Some bring $200; some bring $200,000 with them. The more people who want to play, the merrier, as far as we are concerned. Of course, the big ones usually eat up the little ones.

I think a lot of people will be in Las Vegas for the World Series of Poker the next few years, rooting for me to win. And I'll try not to disappoint them; but good Lord, there are so many top players and hundreds of others who aren't far off from world class. Between the Internet and all the information available now, these young kids sure can play. Here's hoping I see you there, neighbor. Maybe

you can use these tips of mine and knock me out of that fracas
And if you do, all I can say is you were taught damn well.

Remember what I said about being able to shear a sheep many
a time, but only being able to skin it once. It sounds corny, and it
is corny, but it works. Be good to people—treat them nice and
they'll want to gamble with you again, and they'll want to be
your friend. If they ask you where you're going, just tell 'em that
no one knows where the hobo goes when the train slows.

ACKNOWLEDGMENTS

Thanks to the folks at HarperCollins who were foolish enough to publish another book of mine. Josh Behar, Mauro DiPreta, Will Hinton, and Joelle Yudin are welcome to be my guests any time in Amarillo.

RECOMMENDED READING AND VIEWING

Big Deal, by Anthony Holden

California Split, the brilliant Robert Altman film in which I have a cameo

Caro's Book of Tells, by Mike Caro

Championship No-Limit & Pot-Limit Hold'Em, by T. J. Cloutier and Tom McEvoy

Doyle Brunson's Super System: A Course in Power Poker, by Doyle Brunson

Doyle Brunson's Super System 2, by Doyle Brunson

Harrington on Hold'em, by Dan Harrington and Bill Robertie

One of a Kind, (a biography of Stuey Ungar) by Nolan Dalla and Peter Alson

Phil Gordon's Little Green Book: Lessons and Teachings in No Limit Hold'em, by Phil Gordon

The Poker MBA, by Greg Dinkin and Jeffrey Gitomer

Six Secrets of Successful Bettors, by Frank R. Scatoni and Peter T. Fornatale

Tournament Poker for Advanced Players, by David Sklansky

APPENDIX: *Hand Rankings*

Poker hand rankings are as follows:

high card	The highest card in your hand.
pair	Two cards of the same rank—7-7.
two pair	Two cards of the same rank and two cards of another rank—7-7-2-2.
three of a kind	Three cards of the same rank—7-7-7.
straight	Five consecutive cards of mixed suits—5-6-7-8-9.
flush	Five cards of the same suit—2-5-8-9-10 of clubs.
full house	Three cards of one rank and two of another rank—7-7-7-2-2.
four of a kind	Four cards of the same rank—7-7-7-7.
straight flush	Five consecutive cards of the same suit—5-6-7-8-9 of spades.
royal flush	The highest-ranking straight flush—10-J-Q-K-A of the same suit.

GLOSSARY OF GAMBLESE

A.B.C. Ace, deuce, trey. A great hand to start with in hi-lo.

all in When a player has all his or her chips in the pot.

babies Small cards.

back-to-back/backed up In a stud game, the first two consecutive cards that are paired (two aces, etc.).

bicycle Ace, deuce, trey, four, five.

blind Money posted directly to the left of the dealer, before the cards are dealt. There are two blinds, and the small blind is generally half the size of the big blind.

bubble Finishing just out of the money in a tournament.

burn To discard the top card from the deck.

case ace Last ace in the deck.

cheat Any device or gimmick used to improve a player's hand.

chips Markers used by players instead of cash money.

cinch hand A hand that is impossible to beat; also known as the nuts.

cold bluff Having no hand whatsoever, but wanting to appear as though one does.

community cards Those cards placed faceup in the center of the table for the use of all players in Hold'em and Omaha. Also referred to as the board.

concealed hand One in which cards are not displayed faceup where other players may see them.

darken the pot To open before you see your hand; to bet "in the dark."

dead to the pot Cannot draw a winning card. Also called drawing dead.

dogs it Throws away the best hand.

double through To double your chips by beating another player when you're all in.

duck To throw your hand away.

eight in the belly Catching an eight to complete a gutshot (belly) straight.

fast game A game in which the bets are made both frequently and in large amounts.

figuring the price of a pot Calculating how much the pot will pay you, compared to what you have put into it if you *do* make your hand.

floor man Shift boss or cardroom manager.

flop The first three community cards in Hold'em.

fold To discard your hand.

freeze-out Type of game in which each player puts in a certain amount and then cannot quit the game until he or she has either won everyone else's money or lost all of his or her own.

hidden percentage Determined by figuring the odds on making your hand and then getting paid off in later betting rounds. Also known as implied odds.

high rollers A gambler who plays for big, big stakes.

hold over To continually hold the best hand against another player.

implied odds Odds after the assumed result for the remainder of the hand.

insurance Side bets made away from the table on the outcome of a game that do not affect the pot or the game. The bets can be between onlookers and players or just between players.

kicker The card that isn't paired in Hold'em.

lay the lash To make a large bet.

leak Money lost because of reckless purposes.

limit game A game in which you have to bet in fixed increments and may not bet all your chips at once.

limp in Just call a bet.

locked up No escape for your opponent.

mortal cinch A sure hand.

move in To bet all your money.

nut flush The best possible flush (ace high).

open-ended straight When there are eight cards you can draw that will make you a straight.

out of shape When a game's stakes become really high.

outs Cards that will make you a winning hand.

overcard Any card that is larger than your highest pair.

pat A hand that is complete; when drawing is not necessary.

peewees Very small cards.

play back To raise.

pocket Hole cards. Two kings in Hold'em are called pocket kings, or sometimes wired kings.

position Your seat at the table in relation to the dealer.

principle money Money borrowed from one pro by another pro, with a definite time set for repayment.

rail The area where spectators hang out in most casinos. Usually a place for broke players who are looking for a loan.

rich When a majority of the cards left in the deck are winners for you.

river The final card dealt—in Hold'em, it's the fifth community card; in seven-card stud, it would be the seventh card dealt facedown to each player.

rock along To take it easy, play slow.

running pair Two consecutive cards of the same denomination.

sandwich Two players putting another one in the middle in the betting.

shoot up the pot To make a big raise.

show down To show your hand when all your chips are in.

slicker than a wet gut To be completely busted.

snowball An unplayable hand.

squeak To complain.

stash A player's cash reserve.

stool a hand To let everyone know you have a good hand.

strippers Cards with slightly raised edges that can be pulled out of a deck by a cheater or a thief.

table stakes Betting only the amount you have on the table.

tell A giveaway trait of players, which can be physical, verbal, or emotional.

thief A card cheat.

tight player An ultraconservative. Also sometimes called a locksmith.

trapping Playing weak when you have a good hand so as to make more money on a later betting round.

trips Three of a kind.

turn The fourth community card in Hold'em.

under the gun The first seat to the left of the dealer.

up front The first, second, or third seat to the left of the dealer.

wraparound straight draw When you have a draw in Omaha in which there are as many as twenty cards that will make you a straight.

wheel Ace, deuce, trey, four, five.

The AMARILLO SLIMTIONARY

Someone who isn't too sharp:
+ If it was raining soup, he'd be out in it with a fork.
+ That boy is lighter than a June frost.
+ He couldn't track an elephant in four feet of snow.

Something of little value:
That ain't worth nine settings of eggs.

A conservative player in poker:
Tighter than a nun's gadget.

A person put in shock:
He couldn't swallow boiled okra.

A naive person:
He's as square as an apple box. He still thinks 69 is the new highway to Dallas.

A close relationship:

I'm closer to that boy than nineteen is to twenty.

An attractive woman:

As pretty as a speckled pup under a red wagon.

Major evidence that proves a point:

+ That's stronger than Nellie's breath.
+ That's strong medicine.

A sucker who falls for a bad bet:

+ Had taken the bait like a country hog after town slop.
+ What he smelled cooking wasn't on the fire.

A big pot in poker or a lot of money:

It had so many chips that a show dog couldn't jump over it.

After I've lost all my money:

+ Slicker than a wet gut.
+ Enough hundred-dollar bills to burn up forty wet mules.

The chances of an underdog:

Very seldom do the lambs slaughter the butcher.

SLIM ON SLIM

+ I'm so skinny I look like the advance man for a famine.
+ I can hear a mouse piss on cotton.
+ I can see a gnat's keister at a hundred yards.

✦ Sometimes I get more excited than a sore tailed cat in a room full of rocking chairs.

✦ If there's anything I'll argue about, I'll either bet on it or shut up.

✦ I'm from a good town named Amarillo. The population has been 173,000 for the past fifty years, never varies—every time some woman gets pregnant, some man leaves town.

PHILOSOPHICAL SLIM

✦ There's more horse's asses than there are horses.

✦ No one knows where the hobo goes when it snows.

✦ You can shear a sheep many a time, but you can skin 'em only once.

✦ I don't believe in hunches; hunches are for dogs making love.

✦ You can't always win. Sometimes they milk me like a Rocky Mountain goat. My titties get so sore I can't button my shirt.

✦ I'd put a rattlesnake in your pocket and ask you for a match.